I0752678

# HIDDEN HISTORY *of* MIDCOAST MAINE

*Patricia M. Higgins*

Published by The History Press
Charleston, SC 29403
www.historypress.net



*Cover*: Out of the Mist. *David Higgins photo.*

First published 2014

ISBN 9781540223043

Library of Congress CIP data applied for.

Midcoast
Counties
Waldo
Lincoln
Knox
Cumberland
Sagadahoc
Ste. Croix
Island
Penobscot River
Bangor
Lead Mtn
Epping Plain
Augusta
Kennebec River
Belfast
Castine
Waldoboro
Damariscotta
Thomaston
Brunswick
Rockland
Hiram
Bath
Pemaquid Point
Portland
Monhegan
Popham
Damariscove
The Maine
Midcoast
Kittery
- Locations mentioned in this book

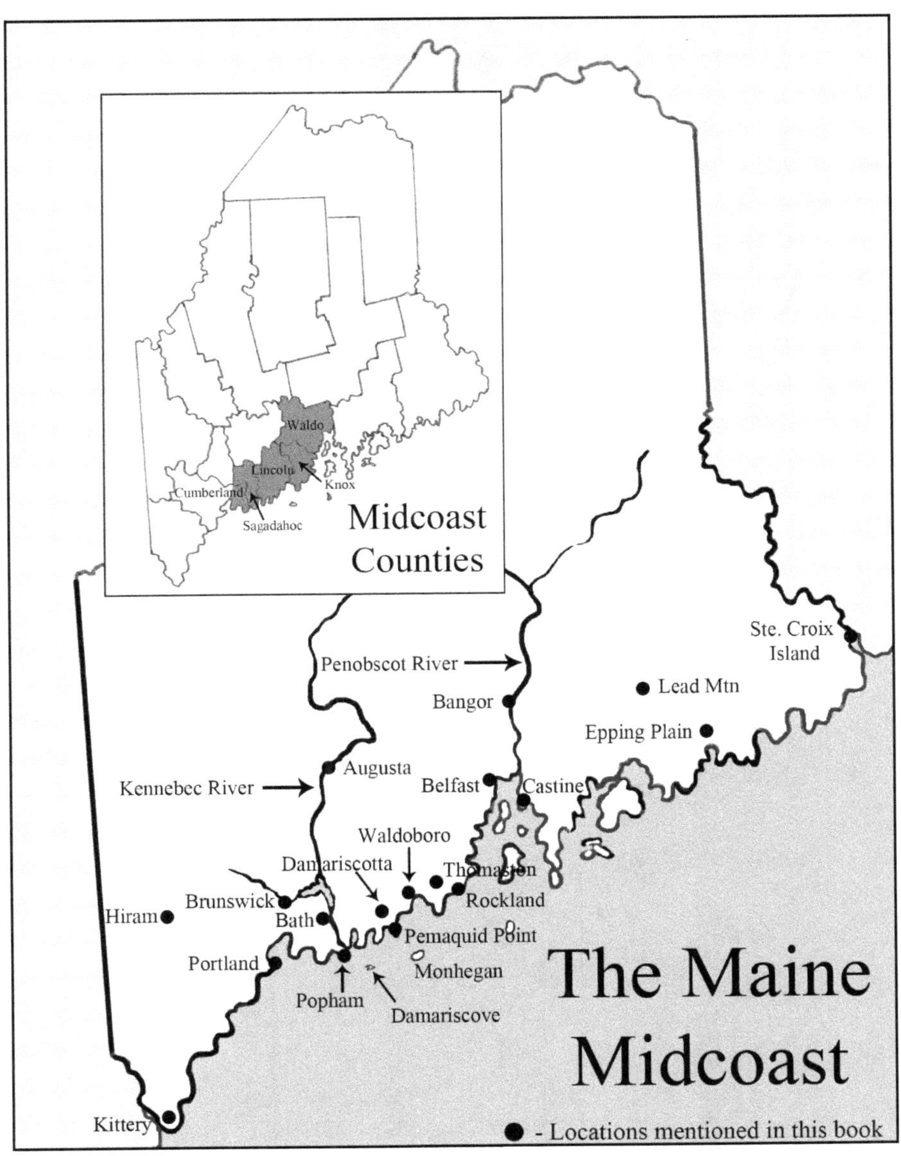

Author's map.

# Contents

# ACKNOWLEDGEMENTS

First off, I must thank my husband, David Higgins, for his support, for being my personal photographer and for collaborating with me on the images for this book. It wasn't easy; there was always one more place to go and one more picture to photograph. Dave rose to the occasion each time. He always had the last words, and they were, "Yes, dear."

The people at the Waldoboro Historical Society were so quick, helpful and cooperative. Special thanks go to Jean Lawrence and her crew for meeting me more than halfway and with such enthusiasm. I have to add that this has been my experience with all Maine's local historical societies; they have wonderful exhibits and volunteer historians who love to share.

Of course, I cannot ignore my various libraries. Over the years, I've been able to borrow a huge assortment of materials from the Maine library system of public, school and college libraries. Many were rare or hard to find. The Maine State Library seems to be able to find me anything that it doesn't already have. What a service! My current local public library, Skidompha Library in Damariscotta, has a nice Maine collection and a wonderful genealogy collection. Where would we be without libraries?

Thanks also to my family and friends for support over the years and to the many people who visit my web page, Mainestory.info, and send me their kind comments, references and stories. Extra thanks go to Dan Allan of Thomaston who caught me onto the *Hattie Dunn* story, without which there would be no twentieth-century story in this book. Without all these people and my students, there could be no Maine stories.

# Introduction

My first introduction to history was most likely far back in the sixties during the Civil War Centennial. *Life* magazine had a wonderful ongoing series on the Civil War that is probably what hooked me. From there, I went on to read John Pullen's *The 20th Maine*. Then I branched out and discovered that history was full of exciting stories.

At South Portland High School, I learned the thrill of the chase after information from Miss Rosella Loveitt, my junior year history teacher. She was tough, detailed and methodical in her approach to history, but at least to me, she was never boring. In the spring, she gave us a page of history scavenger hunt questions to find answers for. The killer question: What three consecutive Portland streets were named after a famous Maine politician? The answer was William, Pitt and Fessenden. That answer was hidden right in front of us. Many knew the streets but didn't see them connected as an answer. Of course, along the way, we needed to learn who William Pitt Fessenden actually was. If you don't know, I'll leave him up to you to discover.

Later, at the University of Maine–Portland-Gorham (now the University of Southern Maine), I had some wonderful history professors who taught me lessons on history as well as lessons about history. From Professor Phillip Cole, Western Civilization, I learned that history is dirty; there is always a seamy underside. From Professor Harry Draper Hunt, Civil War and Reconstruction, I learned that there is a big picture and a lot of steps leading up to any historical event that are at least as important and interesting as that event itself. He spent a semester escorting us through all the events, causes and people leading up to the Civil War and concluded with only one lecture on the war itself and another on Reconstruction. From William Jordan, Maine History, I learned history happens here in Maine, and it is fascinating. You can stand in that certain spot and see the identical view where history took place right in your neighborhood. One further thing I learned in my college history studies is if you can find that one obscure story that the professor has not heard about or, at the very least, has seldom seen a paper about, then it is worth brownie points on the grade of your research paper for the class.

There was no way that I would be able to make a living with a history degree, so I did the next best thing: I became a librarian. I taught many, many lessons to middle schoolers about reference books and information gathering. Then computers and the Internet came on the scene and changed everything about searching and access to information. My first website experience was compiling a list of sites about Maine to assist my students in finding information for their Maine studies class. From there, it was a short jump to compiling and writing up some of these stories for my own website. And here we are.

So this is what I have learned and what I hope that I have brought to *Hidden History of Midcoast Maine*: interesting stories that are not well known or include forgotten or hidden subsidiary happenings; connections to the local community, state, the nation and the world; the whole story, step by step, with causes and effects; and, above all, the dirty, spicy tidbits.

*I*

# Cushnoc, or How Maine Saved the Pilgrims

Maine very nearly won the prize for hosting the first English colony in North America. The Plymouth Company of Virginia attempted to settle a colony, the Popham Colony, at the mouth of the Kennebec in 1607, the same year that Jamestown was begun in Virginia. Jamestown survived, but the Popham colonists packed up and went home after a year. Among other things, bad leadership and a Maine winter did them in. With the demise of Popham Colony in 1608, Maine lost all claim to having the first official, successful English settlement in New England to the Pilgrims, who did not settle at Plymouth until 1620, a good dozen years later. Plymouth became a national landmark and an almost iconic center of the colonial beginnings in the North. The Pilgrims gave us our first Thanksgiving,

The site of Popham Colony (center) as seen across Atkins Bay from Fort Popham on Hunniewell's Point. *David Higgins photo.*

now celebrated gloriously in the kitchens and in the elementary schools of America. Popham got lost along the way, but Maine did not. In fact, Maine and the Pilgrims had a long-standing connection that may have saved the little Plymouth Colony more than once.

## "Welcome, English"

First and foremost, how would Plymouth have survived without Squanto or Samoset? Every school kid knows how Samoset made the first friendly native overture to the Pilgrims and how Squanto taught them to grow Indian corn. But how many know that New England was sprinkled with Native Americans who had been kidnapped and sold into slavery by greedy explorers or who had interacted with seasonal settlements full of fishermen parked on their shores? Both Squanto and Samoset were just such natives. Squanto was carried away and miraculously found his way back to New England. Samoset lived on or near the much-frequented island of Monhegan, where he interacted with all manner of European fishermen, explorers and traders.

Squanto, whose real name was something closer to Tisquantum, is often described as one of the five Indians captured by Captain George Weymouth in his 1605 foray from Cape Cod down east to Penobscot Bay exploring for the Plymouth Company. However, he was really a Patuxet from a village on the very site of the future Plymouth Colony. James Rosier, Weymouth's recorder, described the capture of the five Indians at a place that was either on the lower Kennebec or at Pemaquid. Rosier is also very clear about the names of their captured natives; none of the names, no matter how you twist your mouth around them, even comes close to Tisquantum. Furthermore, over the next year or two, none of the captives were mute but were, rather, very forthcoming with information about their homeland. Tisquantum would certainly have said plenty about the Pautuxets and their Massachusetts home. Even though the Englishmen seem fairly clueless about locations in New England despite their frequent explorations, they certainly would have caught on and made note that this particular man was different. The weight of evidence now disproves that Tisquantum was one of Weymouth's five captured Maine Indians.

That said, Tisquantum may very well have spent time with Sir Ferdinando Gorges, the proprietor of Maine, and this is what leads to the confusion. According to James P. Baxter in his *Sir Ferdinando Gorges and His Province of*

*Maine*, late in his life, Gorges referred to Tisquantum as "his Indian" and talked about what valuable services the native supplied, but according to Baxter and others, Gorges was confused and was mixing his Indians up. A more likely scenario is that in 1614, explorer Captain Thomas Hunt kidnapped and attempted to sell Tisquantum and other natives into slavery in Spain, thus further ensuring the animosity of the New England tribes. Tisquantum and some of his fellow captives were rescued by Spanish friars, and eventually, he found his way to England. There is some possibility that he spent time with Gorges and also that he traveled back and forth to Newfoundland more than once. There, in 1619, he met up with Captain Thomas Dermer, who wrote to Gorges about taking Tisquantum with him

An artist's rendition of the meeting of Samoset and the Pilgrims. *From* The Indian Races of North and South America *by Charles De Wolf Brownell, 1864.*

on a trip to New England. It seems quite possible that both Englishmen already knew him, perhaps from Tisquantum's time in England. During their trip south, they stopped at Monhegan, and Samoset came on board.

Samoset is generally described as the sagamore of Monhegan. This island had early and regular visits from Europeans, particularly fishermen. According to the Pilgrims, Samoset spoke broken English possibly learned from Monhegan's visitors. Other sources, often disputed, indicate that Samoset was also carried away as a captive to England, although this story seems quite unsubstantiated. Samoset either returned to Monhegan with Dermer and Tisquantum in 1619 or, more likely, met them there. Both natives sailed on the Englishman's ship to Pautuxet, where Tisquantum found that all his tribe was dead. This is the period of the Great Dying, when the native population was reduced by disease by more than 75 percent. Dermer continued south to his own death from wounds incurred in an attack by less friendly Indians. His two native friends stayed in Massachusetts, and this put them in place for their meeting with Pilgrim mythology only a few months later.

Incidentally, Samoset may have been responsible for the famous, or perhaps infamous, sobriquet "Yankee." According to the French Jesuit Maurault in his *Histoire des Abenakis*, the Maine sachem greeted the Pilgrims with "Welcome, Engis." Samoset's poor pronunciation sounded more like "Welcome, Yankees." Furthermore, Maine historian Louis Hatch says that Samoset and John Summerset were one and the same. Summerset and Unongoit hold the dubious honor of being the Indians who sold all the land between Pemaquid and Round Pond to John Brown of New Harbor. This sale in 1625 was Maine's first recorded land deed between the natives and the English.

Both Tisquantum and Samoset were guides and translators. A veritable wealth of information on New England, they were important allies for the group bent on bringing English colonization and trade to the New World. The Pophams, Christopher Leavitt, John Smith, Thomas Dermer, Ferdinando Gorges and even Thomas Hunt were actively in pursuit of the best location for a settlement and not just gold, fur or the Northwest Passage. To the Pilgrims, who were equally active in trying to live out their lives on strange shores, information was critical. For whatever reason, the two natives were happy to help. It was a short-lived sweet spot in Native American–English relations.

## "THAT YOU SENT NO LADING IN THE SHIP IS WONDERFUL AND WORTHILY DISTASTED"

We like to think that the Pilgrims came to New England for religious freedom; true in part, but they did not come on their own. They were taken on by the Plymouth Company's successor, the Council for New England, as they settled in the council's jurisdiction. Their sponsors, a group of London investors called "merchant adventurers," were in business, and the Pilgrims did not have a free ride. Contracts were signed by these investors who pledged money but stayed in England and the Pilgrims, who did not have much money but were willing to do the work of colonization. It was one of the early joint venture stock companies. The Pilgrims had to produce, and big returns were expected. That is where Maine comes in. This lesser-known Maine connection so vital to Plymouth Colony's survival was the trading post on the Kennebec at Cushnoc, now known as Augusta.

According to Ruth McIntyre in *Debts Hopeful and Desperate*, the debt eventually totaled out at around £7,000 with £1,200 to £1,600 expended before the *Mayflower* set sail. The Pilgrims needed to find a way to buy themselves out of debt. So far from a source of necessary goods, they were absolutely destitute of the most ordinary needs. Each supply ship from England barely provided any of these needs, but the colony's debt increased nonetheless. The interest rates were usurious, often as high as 50 percent. Regardless, the little colony had to borrow more and still wasn't certain of its fate.

In April 1621, the *Mayflower* returned to England empty. Thomas Weston, the often unscrupulous agent for the Pilgrims' merchant adventurers in London, claimed that although he was able to understand the desperate conditions that the colony faced during its first winter, the investors were unhappy. E.J. Chandler in his *Ancient Sagadahoc* quotes Weston: "That you sent no lading in the ship is wonderful and worthily distasted. I know your weakness was the cause of it, and I believe more weakness of judgement [*sic*] than weakness of hands." Obviously, he did not understand at all. Between December 1620 and the following March, nearly half the *Mayflower* crew and half the Pilgrims succumbed to disease. Surely he knew this from the *Mayflower* captain, but the pressure was applied anyway. Late in the year 1621, the *Fortune* shipped a load of laboriously produced clapboards and some beaver pelts to England from the infant colony. This was a hard-won shipment for the Pilgrims, who estimated the value at about £500. It was a start at repayment that soon met with disaster when the little ship was captured by the French.

## "They Knew Ye Way to Those Parts for Their Benefite Hearafter"

A few months later, in the spring of 1622, a shallop from the fishing fleet at Damariscove Island arrived with letters for the Pilgrim fathers. The Pilgrims were near starvation, as the previous year's harvest was running out. It was a hardship to feed their own people let alone the seven visitors. One letter was from a Captain John Huddlestone of the fishing fleet warning them that there had been a great massacre in Jamestown by the Indians. Huddlestone did not know the Pilgrims but was offering this warning out of kindness and concern. Desperate, Governor Bradford immediately sent Edward Winslow to Damariscove as an emissary in one of their little shallops—they were reduced to begging for help. Winslow returned with a load of much-needed supplies, all contributed by the fishing fleet at no cost to the little colony. This was their first venture down east, but as Bradford wrote, it "had a duble benefite, first a present refreshing by ye food brought, and secondly, they knew ye way to those parts for their benefite hearafter." Today, William Bradford's history "of Plimoth plantation" provides a complete and invaluable account of the colony.

Conditions at Plymouth very slowly improved over the next few years. The Pilgrims had very little idea of how to fish, hunt or trap, but in 1624, they again ventured into Maine with plans for fishing and trading. Apparently, seamanship was not a strong suit either; nearly before they had set sail from Plymouth Harbor, they managed to lose their sails and rigging in a storm and were forced to return home. Dutifully, they made the repairs and set out again for Damariscove in the repaired *Little James* only to meet with another disaster. This time, in another violent storm, their little pinnace was dashed against the rocks in Damariscove Harbor, sustaining a hole in the hull and sinking. Again, they were rescued by the local fishing fleet. The fishermen helped them salvage their boat by refloating it with empty barrels, but this time, the rescue came with a bill. Two expensive repairs made the mission a failure. Later, adding insult to injury, the *Little James* was snatched while on a trip to London by one of the merchant adventurers as payment for debts.

## "Very Well Furnished for Trade"

The Pilgrims gave up the idea of fishing for profit but returned to Maine the following fall, 1625, and began trade in earnest using the corn from their first good harvest. Finally, they caught some good weather and a little luck. It was a good thing because the corn was barely covered by a little deck, and there were no seamen aboard. The Pilgrims were going into business as poor men; they didn't have much with which to work. No matter, Maine was not as agriculturally supported as Massachusetts and the South; the corn was very desirable to the native populace. This little trading mission was led by Edward Winslow, an early Pilgrim leader and, later on, the third governor of the colony. It was the first to sail up the Kennebec; the results were a lucrative seven hundred pounds of beaver. The Pilgrims became hopeful that Maine trade would eventually buy them out of debt.

The fur trade was not without expenses or competition. Others quickly saw the profits gained by this little expedition and sought to cut themselves a piece of the business. The success of the Pilgrim-Indian trade had not gone unnoticed; competition was growing. Very quickly, trade required twice as much corn, and they were hard-pressed to transport enough to conduct business. A price war was soon in play. Realizing that they must spend money to make money, the Pilgrims enlarged and strengthened their small open shallop and fitted it out with a deck. Goods other than corn would also benefit their trade. About £800 of the proceeds from their first trip were used to buy out the goods of the Monhegan trading post belonging to Abraham Jennings of Plymouth, England, and also the salvaged trade cargo of a French ship wrecked at Sagadahoc. They became, in Bradford's words, "very well furnished for trade."

By 1627, the Pilgrim traders were facing two problems. First, they needed to tackle debt repayment. The scheme was to renegotiate the debt with their London investors with a guarantee of repayment by Bradford and seven others, who would be known as the "Undertakers." This little group would take control of the trade goods and vessels and would operate all trade by the colony in both Maine and southern New England. Second, they must petition for a land patent to protect their vital trade operations. Various factions, not just the Pilgrims, spoke of obtaining exclusive patent rights to the Kennebec. The Pilgrims immediately began these negotiations for themselves. Best to be first in these things; fishing rights already marked off most of New England and were causing all kinds of difficulties. Isaac Allerton was sent to England to negotiate both deals.

Problem number one was taken in hand with an agreement on the debt. The settlement was negotiated to £1,800, payable in annual payments of £200. Perhaps the merchant adventurers were desperate to recoup any of their investment at all and were afraid the debt would continue to grow

The Pilgrim Patent
&
Nearby Colonies
1630
Cushnoc 1628
Kennebec River
Sheepscot
1630
Merrymeeting
Bay
Pejepscot
1628
Pemaquid
1625
Arrowsic
1625
Damariscove
Island 1608
Popham 1607

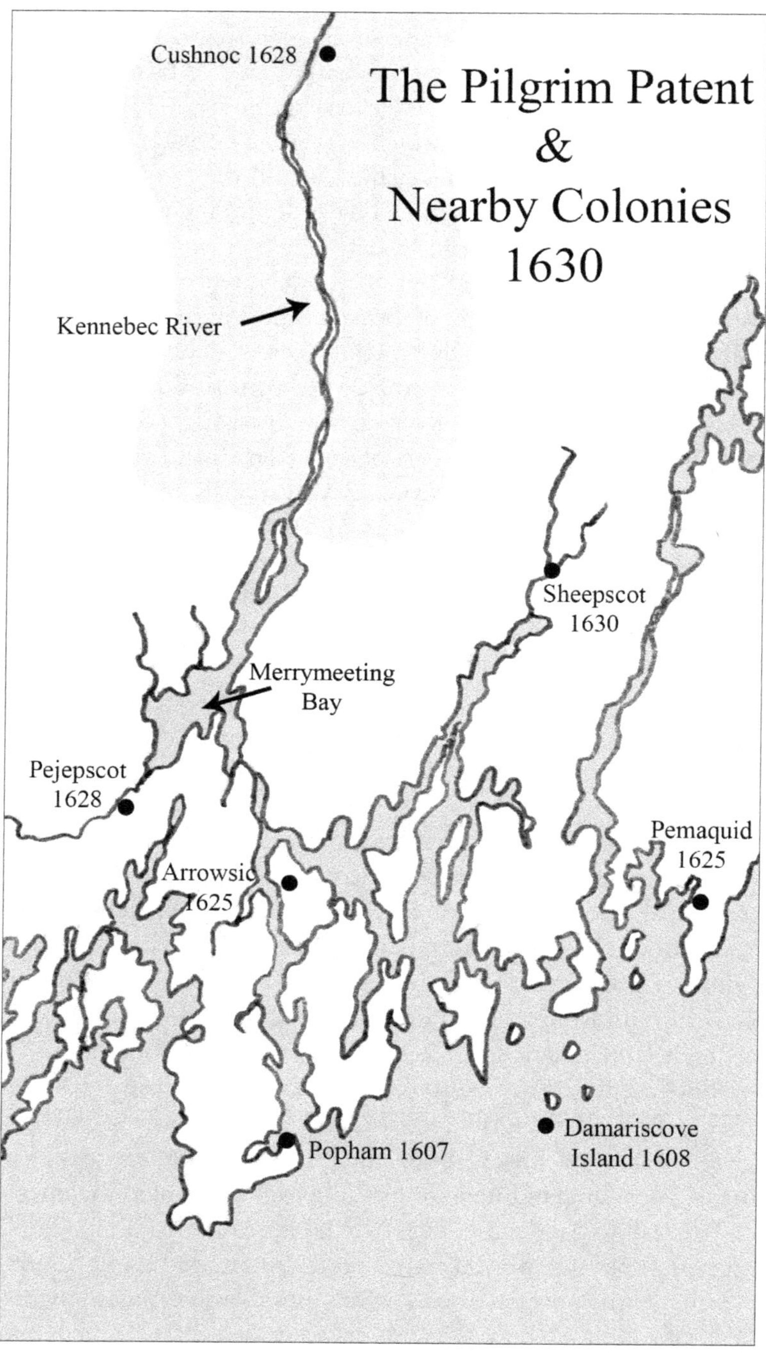

Author's map.

wildly out of control. The first installment was due in 1628. The Undertakers included Bradford and Allerton, plus Miles Standish, John Alden, William Brewster, John Howland, Edward Winslow and Thomas Prence; most are familiar names in the Pilgrim story. The following year, they were joined by four Londoners who took care of protecting the patent on the English side of the Atlantic. Repayment was all but guaranteed by the patent for exclusive trade on the Kennebec, which was the solution to the second problem facing the Pilgrims.

## "IN YE MOST CONVENIENTEST PLACE FOR TRADE"

The Undertakers did not find their first patent for the Kennebec (1628) completely satisfactory, but the second in early 1630 solved some of the difficulties. James W. North in his *History of Augusta, Maine* quoted and described the patent as follows. Not only was it large enough (from "the utmost limitts of Cobbiseconte" to "the Falls at Nequamkike"—a location that remains unknown to this day—and the "space of fifteen Englishe miles on each side of the said river"), but it also granted control of the river itself even though it did not extend all the way to the ocean. At this time, Kennebec was the name applied to the river above Chop Point, and Sagadahoc was the name used for the river south from Chop Point to the ocean. "Free Ingresse, Egresse and Regresse with Shipps, Boats, Shallops and other vessels from the Sea" was specifically granted on the Sagadahoc, while free passage on the Kennebec was denied to other trading parties. It was a cozy monopoly.

It would be particularly important and conducive to trade if the Pilgrims built a trading house where they could store goods and conduct business. It may be that they actually already had such a place at the mouth of the Kennebec very close to the old Popham Colony site on Sabino Point. Historians have debated this hotly in the past. With the new patent, this location was no longer suitable because it lay outside the patented borders.

And so a trading post was established probably in 1628 in what Bradford calls the "convenientest place for trade" near the present location of Fort Western in Augusta and at the time known as Cushnoc. Because the location was described in the earliest accounts as at the head of navigation, Augusta seemed the likeliest spot, although many historians disagreed. The exact location was determined by Leon Cranmer and others in an archaeological dig to be just southerly of Fort Western on the east side of the Kennebec and

Looking across the park at Fort Western. This grass area is the estimated site of the Cushnoc Trading Post. *David Higgins photo.*

on an embankment above a small cove. In the late 1970s and early 1980s, excavations at nearby Fort Western only yards away led to exploratory digs and the later establishment of the trading post's location. By 1987, significant findings and proof led to the general acceptance of the location of Cushnoc as in the yard of the modern-day First Church of Christ Scientist.

Thanks to this archaeological work, we have a general idea of the makeup of the Cushnoc trading post. There are no known historical documents that give much detail. The dig uncovered, as Cranmer described it, "a series of evenly spaced post holes delineating a 20'x44' structure" built using earth-fast construction techniques. Basically, this means that it was a timber-frame

building using posts that sat on the ground or, in this case, in postholes. This was not a technique that exhibited longevity in its buildings largely due to rot, but on the other hand, it was quicker and easier to build than those on stone foundations. Other findings indicate that there was likely a wattle-and-daub fireplace, a tiny cellar and clapboard siding but no glass windows. This was the main building where the small staff lived and worked. Excavations indicate there were other outbuildings and a palisade.

The Undertakers set up a communal trade organization to operate their Maine business interests. Edward Winslow, John Howland, Miles Standish and John Alden figured prominently in the governance and operation of the post with John Howland on the spot at Cushnoc as factor. Howland began his time at Plymouth as an indentured servant of the first governor, John Carver. He became a freeman and an important player after Carver died during that first difficult year. Miles Standish and John Alden, of course, have their own charming little piece of mythology and a connection to Maine via the poet Henry Wadsworth Longfellow. "The Courtship of Miles Standish," Longfellow's classic poem, is totally fictional. John Alden did not propose to Pricilla Mullins on Miles Standish's behalf; Pricilla did not encourage Alden to speak for himself. The only kernel of truth in the story is that John and Pricilla married. Furthermore, neither Standish nor Alden was actually a Pilgrim, although both would figure large in the struggles of the little colony. Standish was hired military help. Alden was a cooper who hired himself out on the *Mayflower* and decided to stay on at Plymouth. Their connection to our story lies more with their part in the Maine fur trade than in Longfellow's poem. Both traveled frequently to Cushnoc in order to discharge their duties as Undertakers.

## "To Prevente a Worse Mischeefe"

Plymouth Colony and its Undertakers settled in to their new role as fur traders and finally began to dig their way out of debt. They were less-than-able fishermen, seaman, fur trappers and even farmers, but trade was going to save them. There were still many obstacles to success and many growing pains.

Cushnoc was not the only Pilgrim trading post in Maine; there was at least one other farther down east. It was more of an obstacle than a rousing success and was undertaken more, as Bradford says, "to prevente a worse mischeefe" to competition. In 1629, without knowledge or input from the Pilgrims, their London investors and Allerton engaged a certain Edward Ashley to establish a trading house for them in the Penobscot Bay neighborhood. It was probably at Castine, but historian Cyrus Eaton claims it was in Thomaston. Ashley was delivered to the Penobscot with a load of trade goods and a few helpers to set up shop. It was a dubious enterprise and put Allerton under suspicion from that point onward. Much to their consternation, the Pilgrims were invited to join this endeavor and expected to provide assistance. William Bradford had little good to say about Ashley; he was "a very profane younge man" but had "wite and abilitie enough to menage ye busines." The Pilgrims were afraid that Ashley might just be successful enough to pull business away from their Cushnoc trade or, at least, do it some harm.

They took Ashley under their wing, joined him in business on the Penobscot and gave him supplies. Fortunately, they insisted on a few precautions: first, he was required to take on Thomas Willet as a partner, and second, he was required to sign a £500 bond for his good behavior. Things soon went amiss; Ashley did not repay his debts to the colony but shipped his pelts directly to London, avoiding any obligations to Plymouth Colony. Then, he was arrested for doing exactly what they had warned him not to do: selling ammunition to the natives. Ashley was transported to England never to return, and Willet assumed management of the trading post. Thus passed the Penobscot post into the unwilling hands of the Pilgrims.

## "AND BID THEM NOT STURR, BUT QUIETLY DELIVER THEM THEIR GOODS"

For a number of years, the fur trade went well for Plymouth Colony. Corn quickly figured less as a trade commodity in favor of a larger mix of items that included metal and cloth, beads, mirrors, alcohol and wampum. This last was a trade system adopted from the Dutch in New Amsterdam. Money was made, and debts were paid.

Then the Penobscot post ran into problems with the French, who had well-established claims to the area. In 1631, the post was robbed by a small band of Frenchmen while the factor, Willet, was away fetching supplies. Claiming to be newly arrived from the sea, the French sailed into the harbor pretending to be in distress and in need of a place to repair leaks in their ship. They soon ascertained that the post was manned by just three or four servants. Bradford tells the story: "They fell of commending their gunes and muskets, that lay upon racks by ye wall side, and tooke them downe to look on them, asking if they were charged. And when they were possesst of them, one presents a peece ready charged against ye servants, and another a pistoll; and bid them not sturr, but quietly deliver them their goods." The Frenchmen sailed away but not without "this mocke, biding them tell their Mr when he came, that ye Ille of Rey [Canada] gentlemen had been ther." The Pilgrims had no recourse; they had to take their losses.

## "TOUCH THE OTHER AND DEATH IS YOUR PORTION!"

The Pilgrims and their Kennebec Patent also ran into trouble, and it wasn't with either the French or the Indians. The Abenaki were eager to trade. The French who operated a tiny mission only a few miles upriver were on good terms with their English neighbors. Pilgrim leader John Winslow and Father Druillettes were reasonable friends; Druillettes visited both Boston and Plymouth. There is even a rumor that Miles Standish, who was a Catholic, visited the little mission upstream to attend Mass. Considering what was on the horizon, this was a very opportune time for trade; troubles with the French and Indians on the Kennebec were still a few years off.

Cushnoc's problems arose with its English competitors who were not particularly happy with the Pilgrim blockade of the Kennebec. According to their patent, the Pilgrims controlled not only both banks of the Kennebec but also traffic on the river. One clause, quoted by Chandler, even authorized the grantees "to take, apprehend, seize and make prize all such persons, there Shipps and Goods, as shall attempt to trade with the savage People of that Country within the several Precincts and Limitts of his and their several Plantacon."

In May 1634, John Hocking, the Piscataqua agent of Lords Say and Brooke and the Pilgrims' competitor in the Maine trade, sailed up the river and challenged Pilgrim authority. As the story is told by state historian Henry Burrage, Hocking proposed to sail beyond the Pilgrim trading post and set up operations of his own in a location that would be first in line to receive Indian traders coming downriver. The Cushnoc factor, John Howland, protested, citing the Pilgrims' patent rights. Hocking was insolent and provocative, saying that he "would goe up and trade ther in despite of them and lye ther as long as he pleased." He sailed past the little trading post to an anchorage just upriver. "Lye" there he did—forever.

Piety aside, the Pilgrims were businessmen, and strong action was required to protect their interests. Howland was no pushover; he set off in pursuit but was careful to order his men not to fire except on his orders. He made a last stab at reconciliation that was met with more verbal abuse from Hocking. Howland then sent two to four men in a canoe to cut Hocking's anchor line. The cable was cut by one Moses Talbot. He was then shot down by John Hocking either as or just after John Howland shouted a protest that if any were to be shot it should be himself. After all, he was in charge and gave the order to cut the cable. Hocking immediately grabbed up another gun and was ready to further protect his interests. Before things progressed any further, one of the men in the canoe, a friend of Talbot's who "loved him well," disobeyed orders and abruptly shot and killed John Hocking.

James North is a little more colorful in his telling. He claims there were two cables anchoring the vessel. After the first was cut, Hocking took up a gun and threatened, "Touch the other and death is your portion!" The cable was cut, and the shooting began. The problem with North's story is that the characters have different names. Hocking became Haskins, and John Howland was transformed into John Allen.

## "CUTTING ONE ANOTHER'S THROATS FOR BEAVER"

Nothing ever happens in a vacuum. Hocking's death had repercussions even though it was brought about by himself and he had murdered another in the process. His crew quickly sailed downriver. They were just as quick to report their side of the story at Piscataqua. Their information traveled across the Atlantic to Lords Say and Brooke and also made its way to Massachusetts Bay Colony. The news was soon "adapted to excite prejudices against the Pilgrims," according to historian Joseph Banyard. Massachusetts Bay Colony governor John Winthrop was equally quick to claim that not only the good reputations of all New Englanders but also the Puritan religion were threatened by the Pilgrims, whose bad behavior would "bring them all and the gospel under a common reproach of cutting one another's throats for beaver."

A short time later, perhaps even on his homeward voyage from Cushnoc, John Alden (possibly whom North referred to as John Allen) sailed into Boston Harbor and was promptly arrested on charges arising from Hocking's death. Now, Alden was at Cushnoc when the fateful event took place; he may even have observed the incident. However, he did not fire the guns, was not in charge of the Pilgrim forces and was in no way, as far as can be told at this late date, responsible for either death. It is true that the Bay colonists were operating only on the Piscataqua crew's story and had no way of knowing the Pilgrim side of the matter. However, they also had no authority to act as New England's policemen. The Pilgrim leadership was infuriated at this self-righteous and self-appointed meddling; after all, Plymouth was a completely separate and independent colony from Massachusetts Bay. Twenty years later, Mainers would come to hold similar opinions when Maine was overtaken by the Puritans, but that's another story.

Captain Miles Standish made his way to Boston with letters from the Plymouth leadership demanding Alden's release. This was accomplished, but Standish himself was put under bonds to appear at the next sitting of court on June 3, 1634. He had not been at Cushnoc at all during the unhappy event. Standish was required to produce a certified copy of the Pilgrim patent to the Kennebec. It was becoming apparent that the Bay colonists had an ulterior motive and were presenting themselves to England as guardians of law and order.

Shortly, John Winthrop suggested that representatives of the three parties (including his own colony) meet "to consult and determine in this matter." The location for the conference was, no surprise, Boston, but only two parties were present: Plymouth and the Bay Colony. The Piscataquis interests stayed home. In the end, a decision was made by only one of the parties involved and by a third unrelated party that had another, completely different axe to grind. According to Burrage, the resolution was brought about by both magisterial and ministerial representatives from both colonies. One imagines they prayed a lot. They concluded, "They all wished these things had never been, yet could not but lay ye blame & guilt on Hockins owne head." Nonetheless, the Pilgrims expressed a certain amount of guilt over the affair "in that they did hazard a man's life for such a cause, and did not rather wait to preserve their rights by other means."

Nothing more was heard from Piscataquis, but largely through the influence of the Bay leadership, the Lords Say and Brooke in England were made to understand the true chain of events regarding their agent.

Although, as quoted in Burrage, the Pilgrims were said to have "imbraced with love & thankfulness" the assistance of their Bay brothers, the whole affair was just the beginning of a souring of relations between the two colonies. Nineteenth-century historian John Abbot Goodwin sums it up well:

> *Plymouth was entirely independent of Massachusetts. The Hocking affair had occurred within her jurisdiction (her undisputed territory), and Massachusetts had no more right or excuse for interfering in it than she had with a case in Virginia or Bermuda. For such a wrong, forgiveness ought not to have been granted without an ample apology as public as had been the insolent offence; but of such atonement there is no evidence.*

The Pilgrims were not totally submissive to the judgments of the Bay Colony in the Hocking affair; to this day, the name of the man who loved Talbot so well that he shot John Hocking remains a secret.

## "The Cheefest Supporters of These French"

That very same year, within a month or so of Alden's arrest, the Pilgrims had another setback with the French and with their Bay Colony brothers. In a story recounted by Bradford, the French, under d'Aulnay, arrived again from Canada at the little Penobscot post sometime in August 1635; this time, it was their intent to expel the Pilgrims. D'Aulnay took possession of the post, liberated the trade goods while declining to pay and then sent the post inhabitants off to Plymouth in their own shallop. The Pilgrims consulted with their brethren in Massachusetts Bay Colony, believing that they would also be interested in the movements of the French in eastern Maine. The Bay Colony leadership gave its blessings, and the Pilgrims hired a ship at a cost of £700 in beaver pelts to drive off the French. The ship, captained by a man named Girling, was accompanied by a Pilgrim vessel carrying the beaver skin payment and also Miles Standish with a force of twenty.

Girling, upon entering the trading post's harbor, began blasting away before he was in range. Standish complained to no avail; Girling was soon out of powder. Standish went off to fetch more. He was no fool in military matters even though Longfellow painted him as a fool in love. Standish

Cushnoc commemorative stone at the trading post location in Augusta, Maine. *David Higgins photo.*

heard that Girling planned to snatch the beaver on his return. Consequently, Captain Standish sent the powder to Girling by a different ship and returned home with the beaver. Girling, of course, did nothing, but Standish had acted to cut the Pilgrims' losses.

The whole fiasco was not over yet. The Pilgrims again placed the matter before their English brothers in Boston, hoping for some real support this time. After all, certainly the French would strengthen their position on the Penobscot now that attack was not imminent. The Bay Colony promised to help but soon waffled. Before long, the Pilgrims discovered that their English brothers were, wrote Bradford again, "the cheefest supporters of these French." Boston was trading with the French and supplying not only provisions but also ammunition. It then became evident that Pemaquid was also furnishing the French with supplies and information as well as supplying the Indians with guns and ammunition. The Pilgrims threw up their hands in exasperation and abandoned all attempts to retake Penobscot. They were well rid of the place.

## "SOME OF THEM, BEING LOATH IT SHOULD BE LOST BY DISCONTINUANCE"

Penobscot aside, the beaver trade was very lucrative and accomplished for the Pilgrims just exactly what they hoped. Shortly after the Hocking affair, Bradford says Edward Winslow accompanied 3,738 pounds of beaver pelts to England, "a great part of it being coat beaver sould at 20s pr pound." The proceeds were applied to their debts. Bradford records that between 1631 and 1635, 12,530 pounds of beaver, most from the Kennebec, were shipped by the Pilgrims to England. Trade with the Indians for beaver pelts was largely responsible for clearing Plymouth Colony's debts.

This period of success was short-lived; competition in the fur trade soon became fierce. Although the Pilgrims had a legal patent for their land on the Kennebec, other claims were encroaching upon their lands. The Indians, with their total inability to understand English land law, were selling off their hunting lands, sometimes more than once and sometimes overlapping other sales. The Pilgrims themselves negotiated land purchases with various Indians to either confirm areas of their patent or add territory to it. The Puritans of Boston broadened their interpretation of their own charter and were seeking trade opportunities in Maine, including on the Kennebec. Everybody wanted to cash in on the success.

In 1638, with their primary mission of solvency accomplished, the Pilgrim fathers decided to abandon their claims on the Kennebec. They probably would have been happier if they had done so. However, Bradford recorded that "some of them, being loath it should be lost by discontinuance," offered to take over the trading post and pay the colony one-sixth of the profits per annum. For the next twenty years, Plymouth continued to maintain civil control over its Kennebec Patent and sometimes held authority over the areas downriver from its patent, justifying its actions as "many excesses and wickednesses have been committed." Trade continued to drop off, there was trouble with the natives and things generally became worse not better.

In 1660, the General Court at Plymouth voted to sell all its interests on the Kennebec if it could just find someone who would pay it £500 for it. A year later, a group of buyers was found that included Antipas Boies, Edward Tyng, Thomas Brattle and John Winslow. These men (and their heirs) held the patent for the next century, attempting hardly more than trade in the area. However, it should be remembered that this was a period of violent upheaval and warfare with the French and the Indians. During these wars, the Kennebec region and often the whole of Maine was largely abandoned by English settlers. In 1753, the General Court in Massachusetts incorporated the proprietorship under the title *The Proprietors of the Kennebec Purchase from the Late Colony of New Plymouth*. Boundaries were confirmed, and settlers were sought. James and William Bowdoin, Sylvester Gardiner and Benjamin Hallowell became proprietors with new towns on the Kennebec named for them. Thomas Hancock and a succession of royal governors in Boston also speculated in Kennebec lands. The Pilgrims may have cleared their debts by laboring on the Kennebec, but real money was made a century later by men who seldom, if ever, visited Maine.

2

# Peleg Wadsworth's Great Escape

During the American Revolution, Maine once again found itself caught between two warring parties. With Montgomery and Arnold's failure to capture Quebec, new America found that it would be unable to carry Canada along with it to independence from Britain. Less settled, less established and perhaps less civilized, Maine was in a precarious position at the edge of a new nation. The British took advantage of the opportunity to invade eastern Maine in June 1779 with 750 troops under Francis McLean and a small squadron of three sloops under Captain Henry Mowat, the destroyer of Falmouth (Portland).

The purpose of this invasion was to build a fort at Castine on the Majabagaduce Peninsula and lay the groundwork to establish a new colony for their Loyalist supporters. It would be called New Ireland, sandwiched as it was between New England and New Scotland (Nova Scotia).

Massachusetts saw this as a whittling away of its territory. Without so much as a by your leave from the Continental Congress, Massachusetts raised an army of one thousand militiamen, as well as twenty transports and nineteen armed ships, many privately owned and not a few manned by sailors impressed for this duty. The ill-fated attack on the new British Fort George in July 1779 became known as the Penobscot or Bagaduce Expedition and was masterfully bungled. In the end, the militia was abandoned on the shores, the ships and transports were sunk or run aground and set afire and Massachusetts was all but bankrupt. But this is another story.

Peleg Wadsworth. *National Park Service.*

The connecting thread is that the expedition brought Peleg Wadsworth to Maine. A Massachusetts native and a Harvard graduate, Wadsworth was an early Patriot who served on the Kingston, Massachusetts committee of correspondence and began studying military tactics as early as 1771. When the war began, he rose quickly through the ranks. Wadsworth was a capable surveyor and engineer, skills that served him well later in life and were equally useful in the military. He laid out the defenses for Roxbury. Later, at Penobscot, he was second in command of the land forces. After Bagaduce, the reputation of almost every American officer or ship's captain involved was impugned. Commodore of the fleet Dudley Saltonstall was court-martialed and dismissed from Continental service. Lieutenant Colonel Paul Revere, commander of the artillery, was court-martialed and acquitted but not before his reputation was ruined. Perhaps the only bright spot in the American leadership was Brigadier General Peleg Wadsworth, who returned to eastern Maine as commander of the militia in 1780, and there our story begins.

## "An Awful Power This, Unless Exercised with Wisdom & Discretion"

Life in eastern Maine was uncertain at best. The allegiance of many inhabitants depended on the proximity of the British. The possibility of trade was a determining and, often, a necessary factor. As Wadsworth himself wrote later in his life in a letter to historian William D. Williamson,

"The Tories from the western part of the State of Massachusetts had flocked into the District of Maine in order to be near the Enemy, & were encouraging the Inhabitants to keep up an Intercourse with them, by Supplies, Allegiance, &c."

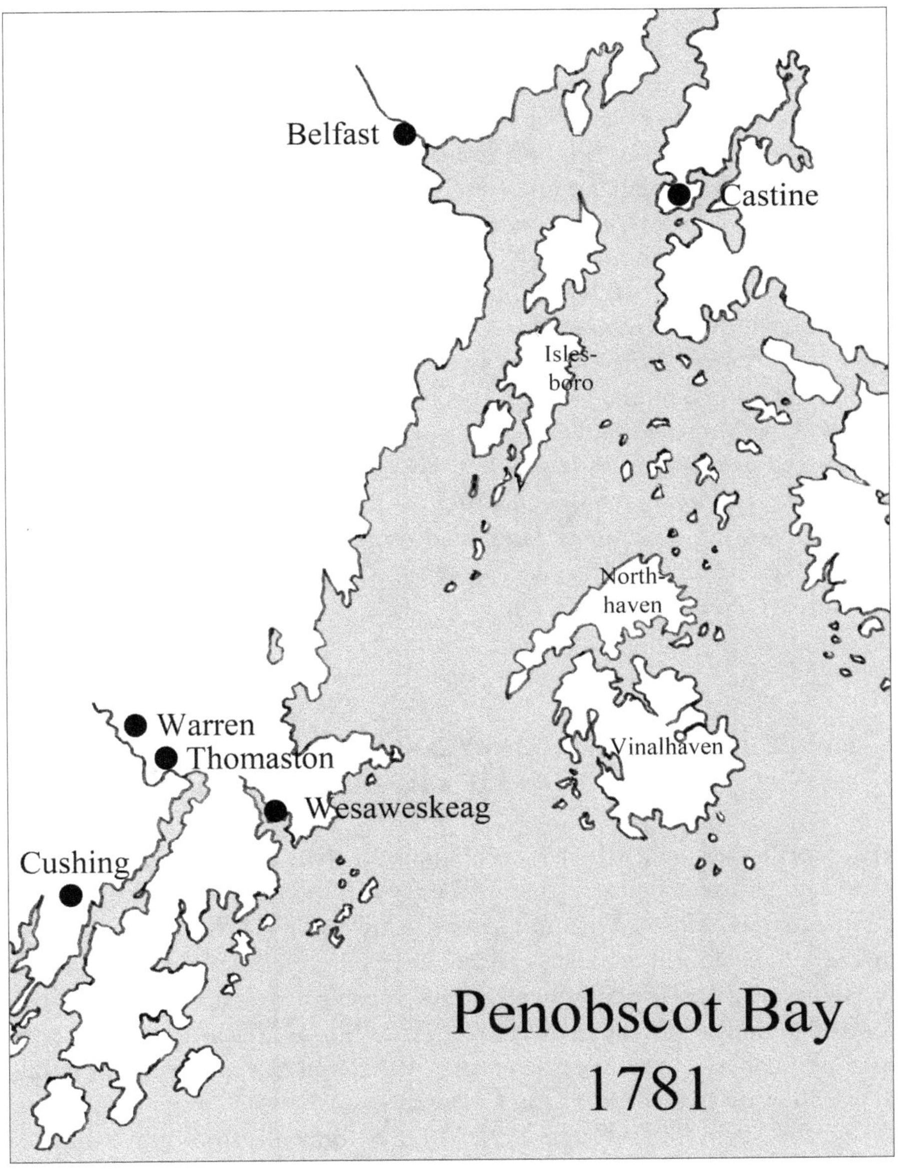


Author's map.

James Leamon in his book *Revolution Downeast* describes the conditions in Maine as out of control. Frequent raiding parties of British troops, or Tories, influenced the local populations to remain passive if not outright supportive of the crown. Patriots were targeted and killed; property and ships were destroyed or confiscated. When Wadsworth arrived downeast in the spring, he found a population whose allegiance shifted with the wind. He did not find soldiers. There were supposed to be some 800 militia paid for by Massachusetts and stationed in strategically located garrison towns. By August 1780, the number rose to an actual high of 552 men in posts between Falmouth and Machias. Food was sparse and terrible; clothing and housing were unsuitable. As their terms of enlistment expired, the men went home.

In order to control the territory, Wadsworth soon resorted to martial law despite his feelings about doing so; he wrote in his *Letter*, "An Awful Power this, unless exercised with wisdom & Discretion." Regardless, Wadsworth did not have enough men to enforce the martial law he declared in Lincoln County in hopes of regaining some measure of control. By Christmas, he was holed up in Thomaston with hardly enough soldiers to defend himself let alone the Maine coast. For the second time, he was abandoned downeast and forced to make his own way out. He wrote a letter of resignation, but before he could leave, the British struck.

The following account is assembled largely from Wheeler's *History of Castine*, Cyrus Eaton's *History of Thomaston, Rockland and South Thomaston* and Packard's *A Town That Went to Sea*.

## "Twice He Ineffectually Snapped His Blunderbuss at Others Whom He Heard at the Entry"

Wadsworth stayed in a house in Thomaston that, as described by F.L.S. Morse in his architectural history of the town, was originally built by a local militia colonel, Mason Wheaton, for his family. When Wheaton's wife died in 1779, the colonel placed his children with relatives and offered the house to Wadsworth. It was a primitive, one-story frame building of perhaps three rooms standing across the road from the Knox Spring. The nearest neighbors were as much as a half mile away across the river at Watson's Point or uphill in the other direction past Prison Corner.

On the night of February 18, 1781, a force of twenty-five raiders crossed Penobscot Bay in a privateer piloted by the notorious Tory Waldo

Dicke. Under the cover of darkness, the ship made its way up the "Gig," or Wesaweskeag River, and set the party ashore about four miles below Wadsworth's headquarters. The party waited at the house of a Mr. Snow until about 11:00 p.m. and then proceeded up Wessaweskeag Pond, across the frozen marsh and then Mill River. Speed was necessary; the raiding party did not wish to raise an alarm. It is hard to imagine in that year and harsh season that anyone would be abroad in Thomaston, Maine, in the middle of the night. However, one Hezekiah Bachelder was returning from the mill at Warren with a bag of meal. According to Eaton, Bachelder was taken along with the party to prevent his sounding the alarm. The party proceeded along the back lots and approached the house from the rear.

Eaton says two of Wadsworth's three bodyguards were on duty in the kitchen; John Montgomery (according to Morse, this was actually his ancestor Daniel Morse) was off duty visiting his father in Warren. Three other militiamen were also on duty that night: William Boggs, P. Sechrist and Nat Copeland. Militiaman Boggs of Warren, the single sentry stationed outside the house, heard a crunching of snow and barely called out, "Who comes here?" before he was quickly overpowered. The guards in the kitchen were overrun when they opened the door to investigate. The bedroom windows were shot out, and the house was in chaos. Startled from their bed in the front room, Wadsworth and his wife, Elizabeth, sprang to action. They were faced with a three-pronged attack: the kitchen, their bedroom and the adjacent bedroom, where their two children and a family friend, Miss Fenno, were sleeping. Elizabeth ran to her children. In all likelihood, baby Elizabeth was shrieking, but five-year-old Charlie slept through the entire attack. A British officer entering through the children's window discovered only women and children and stopped that prong of the assault. Two rooms, then, were under British control: the back bedroom and the kitchen.

The general was barricaded in the third room behind, Eaton says, doors "strongly barred." Meanwhile, Wadsworth grabbed up his arms. He put up quite a fight with pistols, blunderbuss, musket and, finally, a bayonet. He managed to keep the invaders back from both his windows and the kitchen door. "Twice he ineffectually snapped his blunderbuss at others whom he heard at the entry [hall doorway]." He shot at least three invaders; two died from their wounds. (Eaton records only two wounded raiders and two wounded American guards.) Circumstances only came to a conclusion when one of the invaders had a glimpse of the general's white nightshirt and managed to shoot him in the arm. Thus crippled, Wadsworth surrendered, and Lieutenant Stockton ordered a ceasefire. The men in the kitchen ignored the order.

Now here's the stuff from which legends are made. Wadsworth called into the kitchen to ask the soldiers there why they continued to fire. A badly wounded soldier rushed into the room and planted his gun barrel on Wadsworth's chest. He said, "You have taken my life and I will take yours." Before he could fire, an officer, probably Stockton, knocked the gun away. The little battle was over; candles were lit, revealing broken glass, blood and carnage.

Wadsworth was helped into his clothes, and the women bandaged up his arm. The women were left behind with quite a disaster. Hickey, one of the general's bodyguards, was badly wounded in the thigh. He was taken off to a doctor in Waldoboro and later recovered. The militiamen simply went home, and the bereft family eventually made its way to Boston. With great haste, the raiding party made its escape with the general in tow. Two of the wounded raiders were put on the general's horse for the trip back to their ship.

## "[AND] CARRIED TO BAGADUCE WHERE I DID NOT WANT TO GO"

Wadsworth, his arm bleeding heavily, was forced to walk along with his wounded guard. He did not expect to last long but was probably saved from bleeding to death by the freezing temperatures. The party proceeded a mile or so to the house of Dr. David Fales. By now, word was out that something was afoot—a gun battle is hard to cover up. Wadsworth himself was silent under pain of death, but the party was not so large that he would go unnoticed. The doctor's brother Atwood, a veteran of the Bagaduce Expedition, knew enough to go out the back door and hide in the woods. Fales and his sons inquired if the party had captured General Wadsworth, but this was denied. It was arranged for one of the wounded British soldiers, supposed to be dying, to be left behind with Fales. The doctor extracted a ball from the man's thigh and cared for him until he recovered.

Wadsworth was mounted on the horse, and the party went onward to Snow's at the Gig. Here, the British released their first prisoner, Hezekiah Bachelder, despite Snow's warning, "Take him with you to Biguyduce if you don't want the whole neighborhood at your backs." Eaton points out that Thomaston was "lonely, thinly settled" at this time and unable to mount a rescue mission at this point.

When the party arrived at the ship, Captain Dicke castigated the general viciously for harming the king's men. Stockton again came to his defense.

Cannon and earthworks at Fort St. George in Castine. *David Higgins photo.*

The ship's arrival in Castine brought another harangue from the local Loyalists. And so Wadsworth wrote in his *Letter* that he was "carried to Bagaduce where I did not want to go."

## "A Very Severe Storm of Rain Came on, with Great Darkness, and Almost Incessant Lightening"

Undoubtedly, Wadsworth found Fort George in Castine to be quite changed from his previous visit to the area during the Bagaduce Expedition. In 1779, the British had been in Castine for barely a month. Wheeler described the fort thus; Fort George (named for King George III) must have been barely started. The fort was tetragonal in shape with earthwork bastions in each corner and 230-foot-long curtain walls. Built on the highest point on the peninsula, it held commanding views of the town and harbor and of Penobscot Bay. The fort itself was surrounded by a number of separate smaller batteries to protect it from access by sea or land. None of this construction and excavation could have been very far along when the Massachusetts fleet attacked, but nearly two years later, when Wadsworth arrived as a prisoner, things were significantly more advanced.

Wadsworth was treated civilly and correctly as a prisoner of war as soon as he reached the Fort George prison. His wound was tended, and

The only bastion remaining with stonework at Fort St. George. *David Higgins photo.*

he was treated like a gentleman. He ate in the officers' mess, had access to books and writing materials and was allowed to send letters to his wife and the governor of Massachusetts. Waldo Dicke was even made to apologize to him. Early in the spring, Elizabeth Wadsworth and Miss Fenno were given passes to visit the general. The women's escort on this trip was Major Benjamin Burton of Cushing, who had served with the general the previous year. Ironically, Burton joined Wadsworth in his prison quarters a short time later. On the return trip, after depositing the women in Boston, Burton's ship was captured off Monhegan by a privateer, and he was taken prisoner. This turned out to be fortuitous.

Relations between the prisoners and their captors began to cool. It was becoming increasingly evident that there would be no paroles. The two prisoners learned that they would soon be sent to England aboard a privateer. There was little hope for either man if they were tried for treason in England. The men began to plan their escape. This would be difficult. Not only were they in a fort with watches at all the gates, bastions and along the walls, but also there were guards outside their door and at the entrances to the building in which they were jailed. Even the room in which they were confined had a grate on the door from which they could be watched.

Below Fort St. George on the west side of the neck is Wadsworth Cove, so named after Wadsworth and Burton made their escape from its shores. *David Higgins photo.*

For a dollar, they purchased a gimlet from their barber. Wheeler says the man was Barnabas Cunningham, their waiter. He was either sympathetic, mercenary or had little imagination. It was akin to the file hidden in the cake routine. They began to drill closely spaced holes in the wood ceiling. This must have been a fairly amusing sight. Burton was tall enough to reach, but Wadsworth was a shorter man and found drilling holes overhead to be a chore. In the end, Burton drilled, and Wadsworth kept guard. To cover up their handiwork, the men filled the holes with a paste made from bread crumbs. Some problems arose with this camouflage method when butter in the bread paste melted and stained the wood. For three weeks their preparations went unnoticed by the British. The men made good on their escape on the stormy night of July 18, 1781, when, Wheeler says, "a very severe storm of rain came on, with great darkness, and almost incessant lightening." They removed the ceiling boards along the perforations and, under the cover of thunder and rain, crawled through the attic space right above the officers' rooms. The shorter Wadsworth, further handicapped by a weak arm, had a difficult time reaching and crawling through the hole. Outside, the storm fortunately drove many of the sentries into the guardhouses in search of cover. The plan was to escape the building and then lower themselves over the wall using blankets. They even had a meeting place on the shore if they became separated. And separated they soon were.

Wadsworth made his way up the east bank of the Penobscot and across what is now known as Wadsworth Cove. Eventually, he found a canoe and, luckily, Burton. The two men made their way across the river, avoiding a bargeload of soldiers sent to recapture them. In fact, they kept to the woods, avoiding everyone for fear of recapture. After three days of eating roots and berries and of difficult traveling, they reached Warren and safety. Wadsworth soon returned to his family in Massachusetts. Major Burton left for his home in nearby Cushing, but this was not a safe place for an escaped prisoner of war. Burton left Cushing for Boston the very next day. He soon joined the navy and was again captured by the British when his ship was taken off the coast of Ireland that same fall. He was eventually freed and made his way home to Cushing via France and Connecticut.

Wadsworth was not the only Patriot leader to be so ignominiously kidnapped in the middle of the night. Brigadier General and Sheriff of Lincoln County Charles Cushing was kidnapped without a struggle on a July night in 1780 from his Pownalborough home. He was soon exchanged but immediately abandoned Pownalborough for safer territories. In the same month as Peleg Wadsworth was captured, the British sent another party to Frenchman's Bay. John Cayford tells the tale of the Sullivan brothers in his *Maine's Hall of Fame*. Attacking just before dawn, they succeeded in capturing militia leader Daniel Sullivan after a brief fight. Sullivan was the brother of General John Sullivan, who served on Washington's staff. Captain Daniel Sullivan was rousted from his bed, and his children barely escaped from their burning home. Sullivan refused to take the oath of allegiance to the Crown and was carried away to imprisonment in New York aboard the infamous HMS *Jersey*. Hardly as nice as Castine, conditions were so bad aboard the ship that imprisonment there was a virtual death sentence. Sullivan died shortly after his release from the ship.

## "I Had No More to Do with the Military"

His adventures down east were quite enough for Wadsworth. After his escape, as he wrote to Williamson, "I had no more to do with the Military." Despite everything that happened to him in Maine during the Revolution, Wadsworth returned again in 1784 and settled his family in Portland. There, he built the first brick home in the city and led a prosperous life as a land agent and surveyor. Not unlike other high-ranking military leaders (Knox, for example), Wadsworth speculated in land. Within three years of his return to Maine, he acquired a grant of 7,800 acres located between the Saco and the Ossipee Rivers for less than $1,000. It was known as the Wadsworth Grant.

The Wadsworth Longfellow House on Congress Street in Portland, Maine. *Library of Congress.*

Wadsworth led a very political life and became a prominent man in Maine as described by historian William Willis. He was actively involved in the movement for Maine statehood and was chairman of the first convention in 1785 in Portland to address that issue. In 1792, he was elected to the Massachusetts senate and, later that same year, to the third U.S. Congress. He was a Federalist and served as a representative in the six succeeding Congresses. In 1807, he declined the nomination for another term and retired to Wadsworth Hall, his estate in Hiram. There, he set about improving his grant, incorporating the town of Hiram and serving as selectman, treasurer and magistrate. Peleg Wadsworth died in 1829 at the age of eighty-one and was buried in Hiram in a cemetery at the foot of the hill below Wadsworth Hall.

Castine is now the home of the Maine Maritime Academy. The town is full of carefully maintained colonial buildings and well-documented historical sites, including Fort George. The interior of the fort has an interesting modern use, however, as an athletic field. The house where Wadsworth lived

An interior view of the fort's earthworks shows an unusually modern purpose as athletic fields. *David Higgins photo.*

in Thomaston was greatly damaged in the attack. Although it was repaired, it eventually outlived its usefulness and was torn down. The street on which it existed is known today as Wadsworth Street.

No account of Peleg Wadsworth would be complete without noting his famous grandson. When Wadsworth left his Portland home for Hiram, he left the brick mansion to his daughter Zilpah and her husband, the lawyer Stephen Longfellow. Wadsworth spent most winters in the Portland house with his daughter and her family. The famous grandson who grew up in that house was, of course, the poet Henry Wadsworth Longfellow.

The brick house, now known as the Wadsworth Longfellow House, still stands on Congress Street in downtown Portland. The Maine Historical Society Library is just behind it with the new museum next door to the right. Few of its many visitors seem to know much about Grandfather Peleg and his adventures, but all seem to have heard of his famous grandson poet.

## 3

# The Sea Fight between the *Boxer* and the *Enterprise*

"I remember the sea-fight far away, how it thundered o'er the tide!" wrote Henry Wadsworth Longfellow in his poem "In My Youth." He was writing about the battle between the British brig *Boxer* and the USS *Enterprise* on September 5, 1813, in the midst of America's truly forgotten and ignored

"A boxing match, or another bloody nose for John Bull" by William Charles, 1813. A political cartoon takes advantage of puns based on the ships' names. *Library of Congress.*

War of 1812. This little battle, based almost solely on wits and skill, may have been one of the high points of America's fight to retain its autonomy. In a war in which Washington, our national capital, was burned by the British, Maine's little sea fight was a source of national pride. To quote an old sea chantey found in Sherwood Picking's book about the battle, "We had an Enterprising Brig that knocked your *Boxer* out."

## "HERE, TAKE THAT BRIG AND FIGHT YOURSELF INTO NOTICE!"

During the summer of 1813, the USS *Enterprise* was sent to Portland, Maine, as Portland historian William Goold recorded, "for the protection of the coast in the neighborhood." All aboard knew of the HMS *Boxer* and its sister ships, *Rattler* and *Bream*, and of their harassment of the Maine coast.

Only days before the battle, the *Enterprise* took on a new commander. He was a twenty-seven-year-old Philadelphian named William Burrows. The *Enterprise* was his first command. For some time, he had been passed over for command of his own ship to the point of utter discouragement. Fletcher Pratt describes the young man aptly in his book *Preble's Boys*. Burrows served on the USS *Constitution* in Tripoli under Commodore Edward Preble, who considered him to be a most worthy officer candidate and technically one of his best seamen. As one of Preble's boys, he could hardly lack influence with the navy. There are at least three likely reasons for his lack of promotion to his own ship. Firstly, Burrows himself was an odd and eccentric man. His interest in all things naval was complete and totally exclusive of anything else in his life. He was extremely solemn and morose but with odd mannerisms and deadpan humor. Preble liked him, but perhaps others in power were put off by his behaviors. Secondly, the navy was not well supported during Jefferson's presidency. Not only was pay low, but also the general public, which did not support the embargo, blamed the navy for having to enforce it. Many navy men resigned, and esprit de corps was at a low. Thirdly, it is likely that his lack of promotion also had at least a little to do with political payback. His father, William Ward Burrows I, was a true Federalist and was appointed the second commandant of the marine corps by President John Adams. Later, he wrangled bitterly with Jefferson and Congress over funding for the corps. The son's commission finally came while he was trying to resign. Now, seemingly out of the blue, while reporting in Washington, D.C., he was told exactly what he wanted to hear by the secretary of the navy. As Picking, who loved to add conversation to his story of the sea fight, put it, "Here, take that brig and fight yourself into notice!" If not the true words of the secretary, they must have come close to the spirit of the actual moment for Burrows. Now he was out to prove himself.

## "THE LUCKY LITTLE *ENTERPRISE*"

The *Enterprise* itself had no need to prove anything. Its reputation, as described in the *Dictionary of American Naval Fighting Ships*, had already earned it the sobriquet "lucky little *Enterprise*." Originally built as a schooner in 1799, the *Enterprise* served in the Caribbean, where it built its reputation by capturing eight privateers and liberating eleven captured American ships. In 1801, it was assigned to the Mediterranean, where it was engaged in the legendary action against the Tripolitan pirates as part of the U.S. squadron commanded by Portland's own Commodore Edward Preble. By the end of 1803, the *Enterprise* had bombed the "shores of Tripoli" repeatedly, fought and captured the Tunisian fourteen-gun corsair *Tripoli*, run the Bashaw of Tripoli's own ship *Paulina* ashore and, most famous of all, helped the *Constitution* capture the little ketch *Mastico*. Along the way, it picked up a new commanding officer, none other than Lieutenant Stephen Decatur Jr. The *Mastico* was refitted as the *Intrepid* and was used by Decatur to run into Tripoli Harbor and burn the captured and crippled USS *Philadelphia* before it could be repaired and used against the United States, but that is another story. By 1807, the *Enterprise* was back on coastal duty in the United States. In 1811, it was put in dry dock in Washington, D.C., for an extensive overhaul. The *Enterprise* emerged again in May 1812 as a brig, longer, slower and more heavily armed.

Burrows's opportunity to prove himself was imminent. He set sail from Portsmouth on his maiden voyage late on Wednesday, September 1, and put in to Portland Harbor Friday. The air was thick, warm and still, a typical Indian summer in Maine. While in Portland, he took on Captain Samuel Drinkwater, a Yarmouth, Maine native, as his pilot to guide him about the local waters. There were also a number of local boys on the crew. Late on Saturday, there was a report of a brig firing on a ship as it entered the Kennebec River. Normally, this would be a quick sail up the coast, but it remained very calm. The *Enterprise* had some difficulty exiting Portland

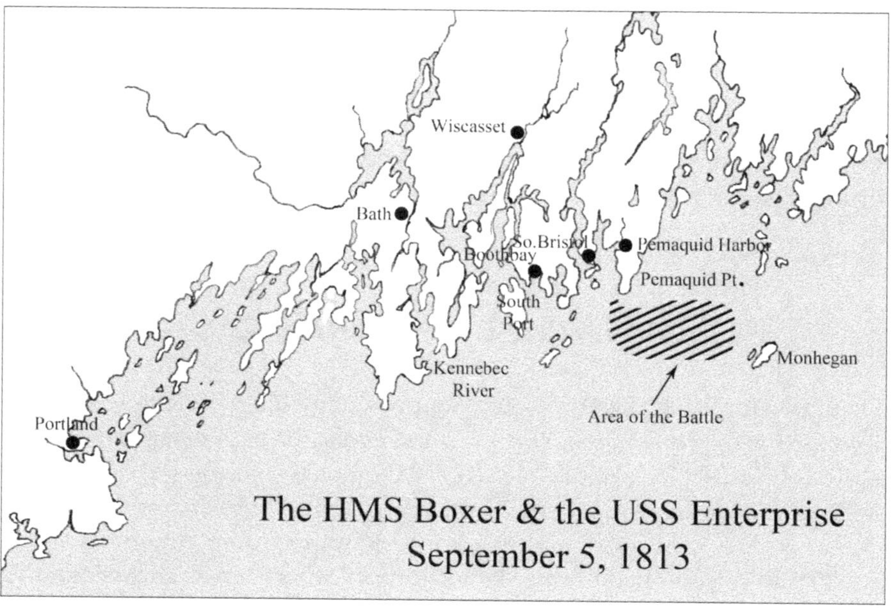


*Above*: Author's map.

*Below*: Pemaquid Harbor and John's Bay showing the ancient settlement of Pemaquid and Fort House (center left) with the Atlantic in the distance, 1906. *Library of Congress.*

PEMAQUID HARBORS AND JOHN'S BAY
SHOWING ANCIENT SETTLEMENT OF PEMAQUID.

Harbor; the coming tide, as well as the lack of wind, was against it. It was necessary to tow it free of the headland using small boats before it could make way. This September weather would continue to plague both the *Boxer* and the *Enterprise* the following day.

## "Lying at Anchor Near Penguin Point"

If we rely on the "official" account of the *Enterprise*'s officers as recorded in William Goold's *Portland Past and Present* and William James's *The Naval History of Great Britain from 1793 to 1820*, volume six—which appears to be based on McCall's official report of the battle as posted in the newspapers of the time—we can put together a decent account of the battle. There are also numerous sources of official information, including government inquiries, court-martial records and logs. However, the all-important *Enterprise* log contains only blank pages for the battle date, as if there were notes intended to be copied in at a later time but never actually done. And of course, there are errors and omissions. Most notable is the recording of Pemaquid as Penguin Point, probably due largely to poor penmanship and Maine's

unpronounceable Native American names. We can likely point to McCall's penmanship as part of this misnomer that extended way beyond this event and down through the years in numerous retellings.

Early Sunday morning, September 5, about 5:00 a.m., Burrows found the brig anchored at Pemaquid Harbor. It was the HMS *Boxer* with fourteen guns under the command of twenty-nine-year-old Captain Samuel Blyth. Like Burrows, Blyth had experience under fire, and this was his first command for which he also had waited overly long. He was the son and the grandson of navy men and was reported to be brave, able and intelligent. The sea fight that followed is considered to have been fought by two of the most equally matched ships and captains during the War of 1812.

On Saturday, Blyth dropped off his surgeon, a lieutenant and a midshipman on Monhegan Island to do a little gunning. Some accounts say that the surgeon was requested to provide a little medical help to someone on the island; others say there were two midshipmen, and the lieutenant was an army officer. Evidently, Blyth was not expecting any trouble; the *Boxer* and the *Rattler* had dominated the area for most of the summer. This would prove to be an unfortunate circumstance, as the *Boxer* would be undermanned by officers when it needed them the most.

At half past seven, as the *Enterprise* made its approach, the *Boxer* weighed anchor and fired three rounds at a fishing vessel, according to the *Enterprise* officers, "for the purpose of ascertaining what we were (as we have since learnt)." This may not have been an attack. A local account, recorded by John Cartland, says the *Boxer* fired shots as a signal to call back the ship's boat that was sent ashore to Fort House to buy some milk. James omits this firing of guns but says the *Boxer* was "lying at anchor near Penguin Point" and, at 8:30 a.m., raised three British ensigns as it set out to meet the *Enterprise*. The American officers also mention the ensigns, adding that the *Boxer* fired on the *Enterprise* as a challenge.

## "THE ENEMY BEING WITHIN HALF PISTOL SHOT"

By 9:00 a.m., the *Enterprise* pulled away in light seas to the south. The two ships were then some four miles apart. The *Enterprise* was hardly retreating. Drinkwater and those local seamen on board knew that a southerly breeze could be depended on by around midafternoon. To his credit, Burrows, who had no experience in Maine waters, listened, but that was one of what was considered his many eccentricities. He was known to spend a great deal of time with common seamen and had learned much from them in the past. The resulting understanding and treatment of the enlisted men won him their absolute respect. Now, tapping into his other attributes, he was quoted as promising to out sail and then outshoot the enemy; but first, he needed to maneuver into the best position. This maneuvering has a lot to do with what naval men call "weather gage." Burrows wanted to have weather gage or to be upwind of the *Boxer*. This would allow him to control the attack by bearing down on the *Boxer*. Being downwind, the *Boxer* could not bring the attack to the *Enterprise* because it would need to tack to sail upwind. This maneuvering took all day. The ships were soon becalmed a few miles off Monhegan.

Burrows spent his time preparing his guns and moving one of his nine-pounders. He had the window cut away in the poop cabin, hauled in the long nine and mounted it there. Some of the crew worried that he was putting it there for protection as he ran away. The *Enterprise* was, after all, headed back to the southward. Pratt says that Burrows told them there would soon be fighting enough.

Finally, around 11:30 a.m., the breeze came up from the southwest in Burrows's favor. He tested his ship against the *Boxer* with two hours of jockeying for the perfect advantage. Around two o'clock, Burrows raised his ensigns and began his approach. At 3:00 p.m., the *Enterprise* tacked to come up on the *Boxer*, which was on a starboard tack.

Then, "the enemy being within half pistol shot," Goold says the *Boxer* opened up with three cheers and a starboard broadside. The *Enterprise* returned the cheers and let loose its larboard broadside. It was 3:15 p.m. Immediately, Captain Blyth took a cannonball through the body, almost cutting him in half, and died. Soon Captain Burrows was hit by musket fire that traveled up an angle from leg to body, a wound that would soon prove fatal. Burrows refused to be carried below and had himself propped up on the deck where he could watch. He demanded that their colors never be lowered, but there was soon little chance of that. Command descended to Lieutenant David McCreery on the *Boxer* and Lieutenant Edward McCall of the *Enterprise*, both inexperienced in combat.

These old sea battles were hellish affairs. Cannonballs careened across the decks, leveling anything in their way. Their speed and force of impact were terrifying. This is called raking fire. Wood splintered under this force, impaling unlucky nearby men. Tons of sail, mast and spar crashed to the decks. A ship's guns often wreaked havoc on its own sailors, who were run

*Above*: This nineteenth-century wood engraving with decorative and patriotic border shows the engagement of the *Boxer* and the *Enterprise*. *Library of Congress*.

*Below*: The scene from Pemaquid Point remains a popular spot for ocean viewing. Monhegan is on the skyline. *David Higgins photo*.

over by recoiling cannons or burned and injured by misfires and explosions. If that wasn't enough, there were also boarding parties with hand-to-hand combat, although this did not happen in our sea fight. Men could be knocked overboard, and ships could be sunk, drowning their crews. Battles experienced from aboard a ship left little opportunity for self-protection.

Moving out in front and across its enemy's bow, the *Enterprise* was able to rake the deck of the *Boxer*, first with that nine-pounder sternchaser that Burrows had moved earlier and then with a starboard broadside that cut away the *Boxer*'s main topmast and foretopsail yard. The *Enterprise* took up a position on the starboard bow, continuing all the while to pound the increasingly unmanageable *Boxer*. It could not return fire on the *Enterprise* from this position, nor could it move to a more favorable one with the damage it had sustained. Within forty-five minutes of the first volley, the *Boxer* had had enough. However, it could not strike its colors, as they were nailed to the masts. To the derisive laughter of the Americans, the British had to go aloft and cut them down.

Blyth's sword was brought on board the *Enterprise* and presented to Burrows, who said, as all the historians agree, "I am satisfied. I die content." He had achieved his ultimate goal: glory. He did not, however, accept the sword but instead asked that it be returned to the Blyth family.

Six men (perhaps more) aboard the *Boxer* were killed and fourteen wounded. Interestingly, four British sailors deserted their posts during the battle. The Americans had three fatalities, and ten were wounded. By McCall's description, the *Enterprise* "suffered much in Spars and Rigging,"

so the *Boxer*'s guns were not totally ineffectual. On the other hand, the *Boxer* was crippled—rigging and sails were shot away, and its hull was peppered by cannon shot. McCall counted fourteen eighteen-pounder holes, eight in a single plank. It is no wonder that the *Boxer* was prized out and not refurbished for use by our own navy.

## "THE GUNS FIRED SO RAPIDLY THAT THEY SOUNDED LIKE BRUSH BURNING ON THE GRATE"

Over the course of this long day, it became obvious to Mainers up and down the coast that there would be a battle at sea. The Harrington militia was called out early Sunday and took up a position at the fort in Pemaquid. The sound of guns did alarm churchgoers up the Sheepscot in Wiscasset and on the Boothbay peninsula. Historian Barbara Rumsey compiled the accounts of Boothbay watchers. People climbed to the tops of hills, which were much less wooded then, for a view of what was going on. Mercy Grover, nine years old at the time, watched from Alley's Hill on Linnekin Neck in Boothbay. She remembered in an 1888 newspaper article that "the guns fired so rapidly that they sounded like brush burning on the grate and the smoke was so dense there were only occasional glimpses of the ships." Amasa Piper, a lieutenant in the local militia, sent his account of the battle as observed from another hill in Boothbay to General William King. Piper claims to have seen the *Boxer*'s topmast and other masts and rigging go down. Hundreds of people watched the battle from shores east of Portland and waited for the smoke to clear and reveal the outcome.

In Portland, nobody heard the guns or could see the battle without a telescope. Longfellow's poem is more artistic than truthful. Portlanders depended on Captain Lemuel Moody, the keeper of Portland Observatory, as they did every day, for his breaking news of which merchant or naval ships were approaching Portland Harbor. He had a system of flags that were raised to denote different ships as they approached. On the day of the battle, Moody provided the people of Portland with a running account of the battle as he watched from his vantage point through his English telescope. The battle ended and the smoke cleared, but it was impossible for Portlanders to tell at such a distance which ship won. Darkness came on. Sometime during the night, the *Enterprise* led the *Boxer* into the port.

The Portland Observatory on Munjoy Hill from which Portlanders heard about the sea fight as it progressed. *Library of Congress.*

Then Moody was able to raise his signal flags: the American flag on top as winner, followed by the British flag for the *Boxer* and a flag with a black ball denoting the British prize.

## "A TOLERABLY FAIR MATCH"

English accounts of the sea battle are a tad defensive; they were not accustomed to losing at sea. Their excuses are numerous. The *Enterprise* was longer and heavier and had more guns. More telling descriptions, according to Picking, were that the masts were fifteen inches bigger in circumference, the guns of better quality and with double breechings and the broadside metal heavier (but not by much). William James, in his British naval history, calls it "a tolerably fair match" at least as far as the construction of the ships goes. Perhaps most to the point, the *Enterprise* had a lot more men on board, and they were better trained. Accounts other than those by the British claim that this was one of the most closely matched sea fights of the times. Sour grapes: the British were outsailed and then outgunned!

### *A Comparison of the HMS* Boxer *and the USS* Enterprise

| | | ***Boxer*** | ***Enterprise*** |
|---|---|---|---|
| Size | Length | 84 feet, 4 inches | 97 feet, 1 inch |
| | Breadth | 25 feet, 6 inches | 22 feet, 1.5 inches |
| | Tons | 221 | 181 |
| | Mast circumference | Unknown | over 15 feet |
| Guns | Six-pounders | 2 | 0 |
| | Long nine-pounders | 0 | 2 |
| | Eighteen-pounders | 12 | 14 |
| Men | Officers | 4 | 13 |
| | Crew | 66 | 89 |
| | Total | 70 | 102 |
| Casualties | Wounded | 17 (4 mortally) | 11 (1 mortally) |
| | Died | 4 or 6 (exact number unknown) | 3 |

Data taken from Picking and James

## "ENEMIES BY LAW, BUT BY GALLANTRY BROTHERS"

Very early Monday, McCall and his prize sailed into Portland Harbor. Many found it amazing that the *Boxer* made it to port at all, and indeed, it might not have if the seas were not so calm. The ships were met by a boat of Portland doctors who cared for men from both ships without prejudice. Many needed tending. Burrows was still alive but just barely; he died before daylight aboard his ship as he would likely have wished.

At ten o'clock on the following Thursday, September 9, Portland went slightly overboard honoring the dead captains. Goold recorded the funeral in detail. The burial procession began with black-draped barges carrying identical coffins containing the captains from their ships to Union Wharf. The brigs and the harbor forts fired their guns. The barges rowed in on minute strokes, and guns were fired at each stroke.

Eventually, the coffins were loaded onto what was apparently the city's only hearse and a wagon made to resemble a hearse. A formal burial procession then left for the First Parish Church and Eastern Cemetery. They went the long way around, perhaps to fit everyone in. Almost everybody of importance in Portland marched: city, county, state and federal officials of any office, elected or appointed; all manner of military personnel, including Captain Isaac Hull (formerly of the USS *Constitution* and now commandant of Kittery Naval Yard) and the crews of both ships; the local judiciary; members of the local marine society; officers of the banks and insurance agencies; and the "citizens in general." Church bells rang, flags were flown at halfmast and salutes were fired. The two brave captains were interred side by side in Eastern Cemetery near the foot of Munjoy Hill.

Ten days following the battle, there was not one but two commemorative dinners in Portland, one for the *Enterprise* officers and one for the crew. The public dinner for the officers was held at Union Hall, where they where fêted by the upper crust and toasted by John Mussey Jr., who would eventually end up with possession of the *Boxer*'s six-pounders. The crew marched in procession to the Mechanics Hall for its public dinner that may have been a whole lot more fun. Many of the toasts given, according to Picking, used puns based on the ships' names, such as the crew's having "enough enterprise to beat their best boxer" or its "boxing their enemies all around the compass." Portland enjoyed its heroes mightily! Indeed, this little naval battle enjoyed great celebrity in America. Notice in the press, songs, poems, dinners and toasts abounded. The following week at a

The graves of Blyth, Burrows and Waters in Eastern Cemetery, Portland, Maine. *David Higgins photo.*

Congress awarded medals to Burrows (top) and McCall (bottom) for their heroism during the seafight. *From* Harper's Encyclopedia of United States History, *1912.*

dinner in New York, one of the toasts was to the men of the *Boxer*: "Enemies by law, but by gallantry brothers." There was no Congressional Medal of Honor at the time, but Congress often had medals cast and awarded to various notable people. Burrows and McCall were both recipients. Soon enough, it all came to an end when Captain Oliver Hazard Perry defeated the British in a decisive and much bigger battle on Lake Erie.

## "A PASSING STRANGER"

In 1815, the two captains were joined by midshipman Kervin Waters of the *Enterprise*, who had languished for two years in Portland and finally succumbed to wounds received during the battle. Waters was just eighteen at the time of his death. The young men of Portland erected an elaborate table-like monument over his grave consisting of five columns topped by a slab (since boxed in). Blyth's crew had a brick cenotaph topped by a marble slab erected over his grave. Interestingly, no stone was placed on the grave of the American hero until a New Yorker, Mathew L. Davis, accidentally came upon the neglected grave. Davis, inscribed as "a passing stranger," had a sandstone and marble cenotaph erected over the grave as a "monument of respect." How strange, and how quickly Burrows became a forgotten hero in a forgotten war.

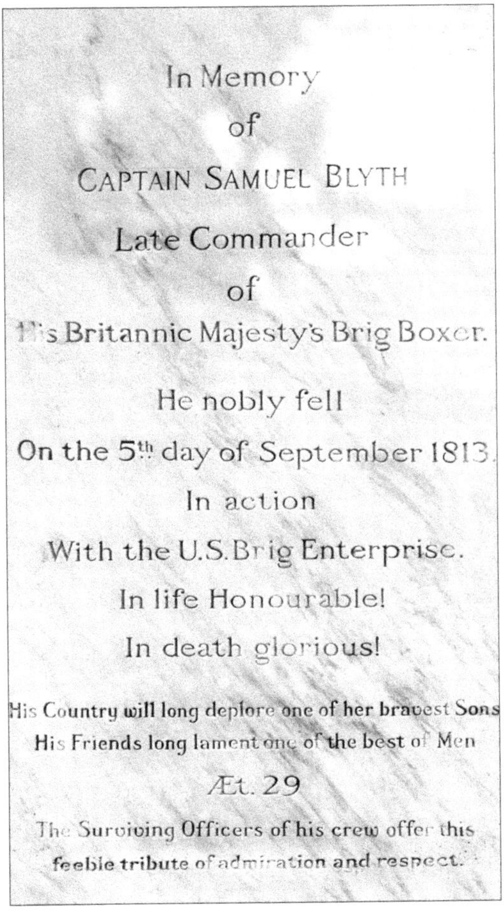

Captain Blyth's stone as seen from above. *David Higgins photo.*

Beneath this Stone
moulders
the body
of
Captain William Burrowes
Late Commander
of the
United States Brig Enterprise
who was mortally wounded
On the 5th of Sept. 1813.
in an action which contributed
to increase the fame of
American valor by capturing
His Britannic Majesty's
Brig Boxer
after a severe contest of
forty-five minutes
Æt. 28.
A passing stranger has erected this
memorial of respect to the memory of
a Patriot, who in the hour of peril
obeyed the loud summons of an injured
country, and who gallantly met,
fought and conquered
the foeman.

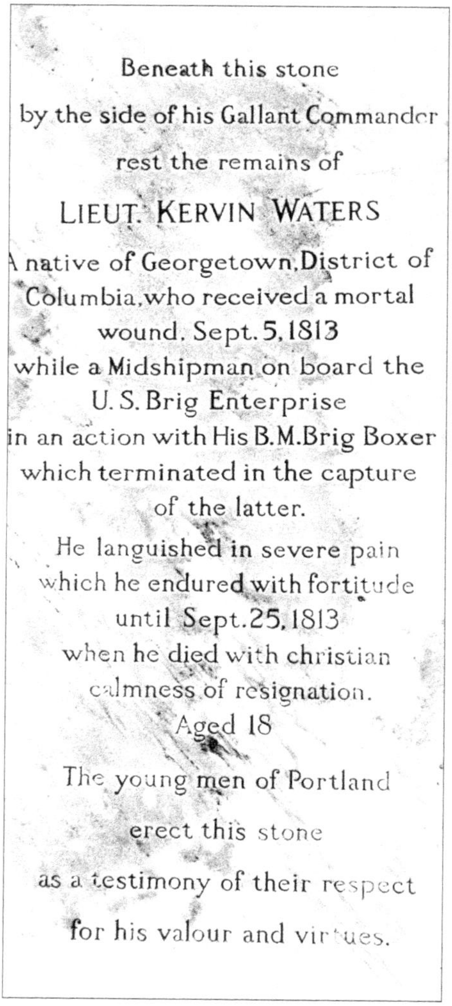

Beneath this stone
by the side of his Gallant Commander
rest the remains of
Lieut. Kervin Waters
A native of Georgetown, District of
Columbia, who received a mortal
wound. Sept. 5, 1813
while a Midshipman on board the
U. S. Brig Enterprise
in an action with His B.M. Brig Boxer
which terminated in the capture
of the latter.
He languished in severe pain
which he endured with fortitude
until Sept. 25, 1813
when he died with christian
calmness of resignation.
Aged 18
The young men of Portland
erect this stone
as a testimony of their respect
for his valour and virtues.

*Left*: Captain Burrows's stone as seen from above. *Right*: Lieutenant Kervin Waters's stone as seen from above. *David Higgins photos*.

## "And Exchange Them for the Paper, Which Was Found in Capt. Blyth's Breeches Pocket"

In all of this, there is a dirty little secret. As with many patriotic stories, there is an undercurrent of ambiguity. As Goold and Picking tell the story, the *Boxer* was not just patrolling the Maine coast in search of American prizes. It was escorting an American brig thinly disguised as the Swedish vessel *Margaretta* and traveling from St. John, New Brunswick, to Bath. The *Margaretta* was, in fact, smuggling much-needed woolen goods and perhaps some other more lucrative items as well. According to Charles Tappan, a merchant on board, there was a tacit agreement that American vessels shipping British goods need not fear British ships; it was a matter of economics. American privateers were, perhaps, another matter; the Embargo Act was, after all, an American law. Smugglers of any flag could be prized by privateers. The *Margaretta* hired Blyth and the *Boxer* to escort it to the mouth of the Kennebec in return for a bill of exchange on a London bank in the amount of £100. Mercenary and illegal, true, but also quite common. At one point off Quoddy Head, the *Boxer* actually towed the *Margaretta* in the fog. It was also part of the agreement that the *Boxer* would fire over the *Margaretta* at the mouth of the Kennebec for appearance's sake. And so an ordinary business deal went awry.

After the battle, it became apparent to certain merchants that Blyth's bill of exchange might prove embarrassing. Tappan says they "employed Esquire K (Kinsman) to take 500 specie dollars on board the captured ship and exchange them for the paper, which was found in Capt. Blyth's breeches pocket." It seems a bit like robbing a corpse except that the money was left behind and only a paper was taken. Lieutenant McCall of the *Enterprise* was responsible for the sealing and inventorying of the *Boxer*. Kinsman was apparently able to persuade McCall to replace the bill with the specie, perhaps by convincing him it was his patriotic duty to ensure woolen goods for the army.

There is still more to this than meets the eye. Who were the ship's owners? General William King of Bath, brother of Federalist leader Rufus King and the man in charge of military affairs in Maine, was a half owner of the *Latona*, alias the *Margaretta*. Despite the fact that he himself persistently lined his pockets with smuggling profits, William King's job was to stop this trafficking with the enemy. Here, he was nearly caught in the act himself by the arrangement with Blyth, but King was a brazen man who pulled off many such contretemps. Perhaps this is why he represents Maine in the U.S. Capitol building's statuary hall.

## THE LUCKY LITTLE *ENTERPRISE* AND THE NOT-SO-LUCKY *BOXER*

As a final note, the bicentennial of the sea fight between the *Boxer* and the *Enterprise* in 2013 has brought a revived interest in the battle, and a number of interesting artifacts have surfaced. A certain amount of debris washed up along the midcoast. Although the British are known to have thrown an unknown number of bodies overboard, there is no record of bodies washing ashore. However, a large amount of damaged rigging and masts needed to be cut away before the *Boxer* could set out for Portland. Boothbay historian Barbara Rumsey says local tradition has it that the topmast washed up on Damariscove, where it was salvaged and used as a flagpole for many years.

By way of trophies, the Maine Maritime Academy in Castine quite possibly has possession of a six-pounder from the *Boxer*. Ken Crocker, a volunteer at Maine Maritime's museum, rediscovered the cannon in storage and tracked its provenance; he believes that the *Boxer*'s cannons were sold in separate lots and did not all end up in the same place as previously supposed. On the other hand, we have long known the disposition of the *Boxer* flag. It was sent to Washington by Isaac Hull and found its way into the U.S. Navy Trophy Flag Collection the very next year. It can be found at U.S. Naval Academy Museum.

What became of the "lucky little *Enterprise*"? It went on to serve its country doing pretty much what it did throughout its service: protect American merchantmen and combat piracy, smugglers and slavers. The *Enterprise* had a long and illustrious service besides the sea fight off Pemaquid. It continued to cruise the eastern seaboard and took at least three more prizes in addition to the *Boxer*. From 1817 to 1823, the *Enterprise* sailed the Caribbean and took another thirteen prizes before it ran aground and broke up on Little Curacao Island in the West Indies. Even then, it was a lucky ship; not a single crew member was lost or injured.

The not-so-lucky *Boxer* was sold as a prize for $11,674.00, which was shared out between the *Enterprise* officers and crew. Prize money for a seaman came to $54.31. The *Boxer* finished out its life as a merchant ship. Kenneth Roberts wrote that the *Boxer*'s bad luck went with its guns, which were used to arm the *Hyder Ally*, a Portland privateer. The *Hyder Ally* took several prizes in the Indian Ocean but never managed to bring a single one to port. But that's another story.

4

# Atticus, or How Maine Ran Afoul of Georgia over a Fugitive Slave

In the spring of 1837, Maine and Georgia nearly came to blows over the "law," the Constitution, abolitionism and states' rights. The brouhaha was another of those little events that added up to the big Civil War. It all started innocently enough. The schooner *Boston* (some accounts call the ship the *Susan*) left Rockland with a cargo of lime bound for Savannah, Georgia.

## 1.2 Million Casks

For many years, lime was a major industry and source of income in Thomaston, Rockland and the surrounding area as they possessed the only large supply of limestone on the eastern seaboard. Packard described the great importance of Thomaston lime to the area in *The Town that Went to Sea*. The limestone was "burned" (actually heated) in kilns until it was red hot and released carbon monoxide. The remaining white powder was packed in casks and sold for use in agriculture or for mixing mortar in the building trades. Nearly every local landowner engaged in burning limestone in order to produce quick lime. Nearly everyone else in the area eventually became labor or engaged in the support industries (firewood, cooperage, shipping). In 1795, there were 35 kilns operating in Thomaston; by 1828, there were 160. By 1845, Thomaston, which included Rockland at the time, was producing 636,000 casks per year; by 1881, the number rose to 1.2 million casks. It was

Shepard Company lime kiln on the northeast bank of Rockport Harbor. Note the barrels used to store lime. *Library of Congress.*

a very lucrative business that made the name Thomaston synonymous with the word lime.

Before the building of the railroads, the best way to transport the heavy casks was by boat. This was, however, fraught with danger. Quick lime is referred to as unslaked lime; this means that it is dry, without added moisture. When slaked or when water is added, a chemical reaction occurs. It gives off great heat and also increases greatly in volume. If this occurred onboard ship, it meant that the cargo and, most likely, the ship would catch fire and the lime would swell, bursting the casks and eventually the ship's sides and hold. Consequently, ships loaded with lime were very careful to seal their hatches before leaving port. Shipping lime was a very dangerous situation.

## "YOUR STATE MUST BE CLOSE TO HEAVEN"

The *Boston* was captained by Daniel Philbrick of Camden; its mate was Edward Kelleran of Cushing, and the crew was the usual cast of local seamen—all very ordinary. They appear to have had no plans or concerns beyond making port in Savannah as quickly as possible. At some point in the journey, the *Boston* began leaking badly, and all aboard were well aware of the dangers. As soon as they made port, the cargo was offloaded, and the *Boston* went into dry dock for repairs. Philbrook hired shipwright James Sagurs to do the work on the *Boston*'s hull.

The actual work was done by a twenty-two-year-old carpenter and slave named Atticus. Having nothing better to do than hang around and socialize, the Maine men became quite friendly with the slave. Atticus plied them with questions, and of course, the Mainers bragged about their home. "Your state must be close to heaven," said Atticus as claimed Fred Hummiston in his *Blue Water Men and Women*.

Sometime around May 4, 1837, the *Boston* set sail for home with an extra soul on board. Sagurs and the State of Georgia would later claim that the Mainers encouraged Atticus to run away to freedom. Philbrook and the crew of the *Boston* avowed that they did not know that Atticus stowed away on their schooner until they were well north of Georgia. Surely, somebody knew he was on board, but by the time Atticus's presence was common knowledge, it was "too late" to turn back. Besides, the Mainers liked the young black man and promised to help him find work in Maine.

In the meantime, Sagurs made a fast connection between his missing property and the Maine vessel. He was furious, dangerous and armed with

The only remaining building of the Knox estate in Thomaston is now the Thomaston Historical Society. The barn and mansion, originally nearby, are long gone. *David Higgins photo.*

two navy pistols. He quickly set out in pursuit of the Maine vessel in a hired ship. The *Boston* had no idea it was being run down, and it just continued on its merry way into its homeport at Rockland (called East Thomaston at the time). Mate Kelleran took Atticus home with him to Cushing.

The trip up the coast did nothing for Sagurs's fit of temper. Upon landing in Rockland, he quickly had a warrant sworn out. Deputy Sheriff D.N. Piper rode down to Cushing to Kelleran's farm to serve it. The locals were one step ahead of him. Piper searched all the houses in Cushing except the one where Atticus was hiding. It is highly likely that Sagurs felt that he was being accorded less than full cooperation by all involved. He was nearly apoplectic. He vowed that when his slave was found he would, in Hummiston's words, "skin that boy alive." This hardly endeared him to the locals. Sagurs's next action was to issue a twenty-dollar reward for the return of his property. There is always someone who can be bought. Two local men, posing as friends, told the frightened Atticus that they would take him to the local Underground Railroad station (supposedly) on the Knox estate. Instead, they turned him over to the sheriff and Sagurs. The next morning, Sagurs and his property were on their way back to Savannah, but the slaveholder was not done with the state of Maine.

## "ALL MEN BORN FREE AND EQUAL"

Sagurs loaded his property aboard his hired ship before an indignant and vocal crowd at East Thomaston. This local population was experiencing their first real exposure on their own home ground to southern slavery, blacks and slaveholders. It must have made a less-than-favorable impression. However, it is important to realize that Maine had a past history of slavery itself and that Maine was part of a country and a region that was coming to an understanding of slavery as a moral and political issue of great magnitude.

Mainers owned slaves throughout the colonial era, but in reality, according to Miriam Thomas, slaves were most likely to be found in the larger and more settled towns where the wealthiest populations lived. Most Mainers lived a subsistence lifestyle and depended on large families for labor. Indentured servants were more likely to be found than black slaves. Her population counts indicate that, in 1753, there were 24 slaves in York, 35 in Kittery, 21 in Falmouth (Portland), 22 in Berwick, 14 in

Harpswell, 12 in Biddeford and smaller numbers in towns like Gorham, Wells and Brunswick. Louis Hatch wrote in *Maine: A History* that in 1764, there were 23,686 white and 322 black residents in Maine, a small percentage compared to other colonies.

Other than Sir William Pepperell of Kittery, who, in his time, owned more slaves than any other Mainer, most slaveholders owned only one or two slaves, who generally worked in the master's house. Again, according to Thomas, they were almost treated as family members. Slaves were baptized and married in local churches but often sat only in the back pews. Their testimony could be given in a court of law; they might own property and were often buried in the family cemetery plots. It was even possible to buy one's freedom or earn it by good service to a fair-minded master. In all likelihood, a Maine slave's status could be perceived as better than slaves elsewhere just because there were fewer of them.

Thomas was careful to point out that it is important to remember now that these people were property, and they were treated as such. There is considerable evidence of this in the wills of Maine people that list a "negro wench" or a "negro man," often unnamed, in the lists of household property and livestock. And slavery was no less cruel in Maine than elsewhere. Auction advertisements listed black slaves. Rewards were posted for runaways. The children of slaves were sold away from their homes and families with no remorse; it was the custom.

By the time of the *Boston*'s voyage, slavery had not existed in Maine for more than fifty years. Massachusetts (and therefore the Province of Maine) abolished slavery in the 1780s after it adopted a new constitution declaring "all men born free and equal." For Maine, this act was underscored by the Missouri Compromise that admitted Maine to the Union in 1820 as a free state. Our statehood was balanced by the admission of Missouri as a slave state, thus maintaining the parity that the South demanded.

Although Maine was a free state, we must also acknowledge that Mainers were involved in activities that perpetuated or took monetary advantage of slavery. First, Maine ships participated in the Triangle Trade that capitalized on goods produced by slave labor both inside the United States and in the islands to our south. This trade was not limited to products but also included trade in slaves between Africa and the Indies and between the Indies and the States. Despite our denials, Mainers did profit mightily from the Black Ivory Trade, both before and after the slave trade was forbidden by act of Congress. Not allowing slavery in the home state did not equate with not making profits based on slavery in other geographical areas. Perhaps this economic connection as well as a small exposure to black people and to slavery itself brought about ambivalence in Mainers to "the peculiar institution."

## "Provided They Are Let Alone by us in the North"

During the 1830s, a number of events and movements occurred that influenced how Mainers viewed slavery. Many were highly publicized and debated. Abolitionist firebrand William Lloyd Garrison made a speaking tour of Maine in 1832, causing a great deal of dissension as well as

This woodcut image of a slave in chains appeared on the 1837 broadside publication of John Greenleaf Whittier's antislavery poem "Our Countrymen in Chains," sold by the American Antislavery Society. *Library of Congress.*

discussion both within and between the abolitionist and anti-abolitionist factions. The American Antislavery Society was formed in Philadelphia in 1833; within the year, there were auxiliary organizations in Maine. The national, state and local organizations were soon actively engaged in antislavery activities and propaganda.

Mainers, particularly from coastal areas whose prosperity depended on trade with the South, were likely to oppose the abolitionists. They might not agree with slavery, but they were more inclined to mind their own business. Many agreed with reportage in 1833 in the *Argus* that stated there were indications that the South "might seize upon the most trifling provocations of a rupture of the Union of States" but would also abolish slavery in due course on its own "provided they are let alone by us in the North." This was the opinion of the Whig Party and its media. It also was the predominant thread in statements made at huge anti-abolition meetings held from Portland to Bangor and is a fair indication of many Mainers' opinions in the early 1830s.

Disagreement on slavery and abolition was not always this agreeable. In 1836, the mayor of Portland rescinded permission for the Antislavery Society to meet in city hall and expressed doubt that the law would be able to protect the abolitionists from their fellow Mainers. The meeting, rescheduled at the Quaker meetinghouse, was mobbed, but despite catcalls, stones and clubs, it was held. As Hatch described it, these anti-abolition mobs were not uncommon. In 1838, the Maine House of Representatives also denied the society the use of its hall for a meeting. That same year, Brunswick struggled mightily with the slavery issue. At first, in a coup by anti-abolitionists at a public meeting, the townspeople voted against interference with slavery and, unfortunately, against free speech and public discussion of the issue. Machias voted by a large majority that "it is unconstitutional and inexpedient to form societies in non-slaveholding States for the immediate abolition of slavery in slaveholding States." Even so, public opinion was beginning to be swayed by discussion and information promulgated by a massive effort on the part of the antislavery societies.

Meanwhile, the South was hardening its position in regards to slavery and abolitionism. In fact, it engaged in a number of activities that pushed the people of Maine and other northern states into line with the more radical abolition philosophies. The abolition of slavery in the nineteenth century became a divisive and self-righteous issue on the magnitude of the abortion issue of today.

## "To Avoid All Interference and Attempts to Interfere, and All Manifestations of Any Intention or Wish to Interfere"

States in both the North and the South were beginning to engage in punitive actions regarding slavery. Such actions demanded the recognition of a state's right to legislate and uphold laws within its borders and at the same time absolutely infuriate opposing states. For example, Massachusetts ruled in 1836 that any slave brought inside its borders was free. Georgia put a $5,000 bounty on Garrison's head for his activities. Congress passed the "Gag Rule" that forbade members from accepting or even discussing antislavery petitions. Freedom of speech was in danger.

The southern states of Virginia, North and South Carolina, Georgia and Alabama even demanded that the northern states suppress antislavery newspapers within their own boundaries. Louis Hatch described the resulting discussion as follows. In 1836, the Maine legislature referred the request to committee. Based on the results of the large number of anti-abolition meetings being held around the state at that time, the committee report stated that, because Maine had no slavery, it was a subject in which the state had no interest. The committee "resolved, that it was the bound

"Abolition Frowned Down," an 1839 satire on the gag rule in the House of Representatives depicting a southern representative scowling at a frustrated John Quincy Adams. *Library of Congress.*

and sacred duty of good citizens of every state carefully and scrupulously to avoid all interference and attempts to interfere, and all manifestations of any intention or wish to interfere, with the peculiar interests, concerns, laws and domestic policy of every other State in the Union." After establishing that the people of the state of Maine were united in this opinion so solidly that it was no longer a topic of discussion, the committee concluded, "In consideration of the fact that no abolition paper is printed in Maine, your committee would deem any legislation on the subject as uncalled for, unwise, and inexpedient as tending to excite discussion which has subsided." And so, in a backhanded way, free speech was maintained. Events continued to proceed toward the abolitionists' goal.

## "Will the State of Maine, Under Circumstances and in Violation of Her Duty to Her Sister State, Persist in Refusing?"

Maine state historian Henry Burrage made a brave attempt to get the tangled aftermath of Atticus's story straight in his *Maine Historical Memorials*. The back and forth of legal briefs soon became quite convoluted. Upon returning to Georgia, James Sagurs pursued his own private vendetta against Maine. Sagurs swore out a complaint against Philbrick and Kelleran and sent two Georgia lawmen to Maine to fetch the men as fugitives from justice back to Georgia. The two men were charged with an attempt to "feloniously inveigle, steal, take and carry away, without the limits of the state of Georgia, a negro man slave named Atticus." The captain and mate could not be found, and the lawmen returned empty-handed. Now, Sagurs complained to the governor of Georgia, William Schley. He wanted justice, and the governor obliged by letter on June 21, 1837, to the governor of Maine demanding the *Boston*'s officers be brought to Georgia for justice. Schley cited, among other things, violation of the (first) Fugitive Slave Act of 1793. Robert Dunlap, the Maine governor (and the next two succeeding governors), refused to allow the men to be extradited. Tempers flared in both states.

As Burrage continued, Dunlap waited until mid-August to decline Schley's demand. Perhaps, he hoped that people would calm down. In his reply, Dunlap argued some fine points of law in his refusal. He claimed that the proposed arrest warrant did not specifically cite and describe the supposed felonies committed by the two Mainers, nor was the allegation sworn to be true. Sagurs stated only that he believed the information to be true. Technicalities, true, but Dunlap did not feel there was probable cause. Incensed, Schley responded almost immediately in his best legalese that his paperwork was, most certainly, in order and his meaning clear. He finished up with, "Will the state of Maine, under circumstances and in violation of her duty to her sister state, persist in refusing to obey the constitution and the law of the United States?" Dunlap did not respond to the second letter. Clearly, Maine did not expect that justice would be served in Georgia.

Schley and, indeed, all of Georgia were highly offended by Governor Dunlap's refusal. Georgian newspapers whipped up a fury over the issue, demanding that southern ports be closed to Maine shipping and that Mainers in Georgia be arrested and held hostage until Philbrick and Kelleran were brought to justice. Schley petitioned the president, Congress and all the states claiming that Georgia's rights and the Constitution had been violated. In addition, the state legislature took up discussion of a bill that banned Maine ships.

However, Georgia could not stand on the Constitution and also demand a nonintercourse law against another state as this, in itself, was clearly unconstitutional. Instead, Georgia passed a number of vitriolic resolutions setting a course that almost hinted at the possibility of secession if Maine did not give up its felons. Mainers poked fun at the original bill from afar. Even the grammar of the bill drew fire. Packard recorded that a Thomaston newspaperman wrote, "If it had passed any vessel violating the law was to be indicted and, if convicted, imprisoned in the penitentiary at hard labor. What kind of cells must they have in the Georgia penitentiary to receive a ship of 500 tons? And to what kind of hard labor would they put a ship if convicted?" Georgia did not pass its bill. Even so, it is unlikely many Maine ships ventured into Georgian ports for a time.

## "I Am Persuaded That the Present Apparent Feeling in Our Sister State Will Soon Yield to Juster Views"

Continuing with Burrage's chain of events, by spring 1838, Georgia's new governor, George R. Gilmore, returned with a new, true bill of indictment charging Philbrook and Kelleran with simple larceny. Maine's new governor,

Edward Kent, waited until the end of June to respond. "Whenever a citizen of this state is demanded as a fugitive from justice to be delivered up to be transported to a foreign tribunal, to be tried before unknown judges...," wrote Kent, "it was his duty to fully investigate the case and indictment in terms of the intention of the Constitution and not just its literal meaning." Without any regard to the "peculiar" relationship of the case to the slavery issue and based solely on the constitutional issues, Kent declined to return the two men to Georgia. Gilmore was not impressed and fired back another diatribe. Kent referred the matter to the legislature, which took no action but referred the whole mess back to the governor. Gilmore declared:

> *The conduct of the Legislature of Maine, and the previous conduct of Governor Dunlap and Governor Kent, prove conclusively that the opposition to the institution of slavery is so great among the people of that state, that their public authorities are prevented from obeying the injunctions of the constitution of the United States.*

He therefore felt justified in treating any Mainer who "may come within the jurisdiction of this state, on board of any vessel as owners, officers, or mariners...as doing so with the intent to commit the crime of seducing negro slaves from their owners."

Gilmore's certainty of Maine's united position on slavery was less than accurate. As mentioned previously, the Maine House of Representatives refused the use of its hall to the Antislavery Society in 1838. It was also a time of increasing ambiguity on the "peculiar" issue; the Maine House passed a resolution that claimed Congress could and should abolish slavery in the District of Columbia. It was defeated in the Maine Senate by one vote.

Also in that same year, and perhaps by connection to the *Boston* affair, Hatch writes that a law was passed in Maine that imposed a jail sentence and/or fine on anyone who without lawful authority aided in the seizure of a fugitive slave. So much for a potential repeat of the greed and reward that led to Atticus's betrayal by the two Mainers and his subsequent recapture. During this same period, the Maine legislature was just as likely to refer or table petitions regarding slavery issues to the 1897 legislature. Despite calls that such action was insulting and derogatory, the Maine legislature was clearly feeling beleaguered by the slavery issue.

The disagreement raged round and round for years before it fizzled out. A third Maine governor, John Fairfield, mentioned the controversy in his annual message to his legislature in 1840, calling the constitutional debate

Portraits of the three Maine governors involved in the long-term dispute with Georgia over fugitive slaves. *State of Maine. Clockwise from top, left*: Robert Dunlap, Edward Kent and John Fairfield.

an "honest difference of opinion" between Maine and Georgia. He felt that Governor Gilmore was speaking unofficially in his threats against Mainers. As Burrage recorded, Fairfield concluded, "I am persuaded that the present apparent feeling in our sister state will soon yield to juster views; and that no root of bitterness will be permitted to spring between the two states."

Four years later, Fairfield perhaps felt differently about the lasting effects of the controversy. In 1844, then Senator Fairfield was a popular choice for the Democratic vice president. His name was violently opposed on account of the dispute between Maine and Georgia. His course of action while governor operated against him in the South, and the nomination went to a Pennsylvanian. And so George M. Dallas, and not Fairfield, became James Polk's vice president in 1845.

## "I Went There Once"

Further information on Atticus and his fate can be gleaned from Burrage's account of the affair. It's hard to tell at this point in time whether the following are factual or just good stories. Thomaston captain Edmund Webb of the *Tallyrand* was piloted into Savannah Harbor some years after the Civil War by a man who claimed to have been the captain of Sagurs's pursuit ship. He told Webb that Sagurs was a cruel master and treated Atticus savagely on the trip back to Savannah. He also told Webb that Atticus was a caulker who made good money for his master.

Feb. 25, 1865.] FRANK LESLIE'S ILLUSTRATED NEWSPAPER. 357

Busy Savannah Harbor from *Frank Leslie's Illustrated Newspaper*, February 25, 1865. *Library of Congress.*

In another story, Captain Eugene W. Cookson, Captain Philbrook's grandson, claimed to have been approached by an "old colored man" who was boss of a gang of stevedores in Savannah Harbor. The old man, who was going by a different name, claimed to be the slave Atticus. He (allegedly) said, "I hear you are from Maine. I went there once in a vessel whose master was Captain Daniel Philbrook. I was a slave then." Cookson claimed to have had quite a conversation with the former Atticus in which the old man professed to have a soft spot for the state of Maine. A little math warns us to take this second story with a grain of salt. Cookson claims this event happened around the turn of the century, and that would put this old man's age at above eighty years. A little long of the tooth to be bossing stevedores, but Mainers have a reputation for embroidering a good story!

5

# Jonathan Cilley

## *Maine Martyr to the Code Duello*

On February 24, 1838, Maine representative Jonathan Cilley was shot down in a duel at the infamous Bladensburg dueling grounds in Maryland just outside Washington, D.C. It is the event that brought about the official (but not the actual) end to dueling by action of Congress. More important, it is one of the long chain of events that led to the Civil War.

### "We Are a Nation of Murderers, While We Tolerate and Reward the Perpetrators of the Crime"

Dueling has a romantic image. Dashing swordsmen with flowing sashes slicing their way up and down granite stairways. Handsome gentlemen with matched pistols fighting over the honor (or love) of a beautiful lady. Romantic? Hardly! A duel was more likely fought by two men over petty, misconstrued or imperceptible slights to the honor of one or the other. Testosterone and what seems today to be a silly set of rules forced people into positions from which they felt they could not back down. The keyword here is purported to be "honor."

The word "duel" derives from the Latin *duo* (two) and *bellem* (war). The meaning is obvious; the act can easily be traced back to medieval days of chivalry and beyond. The Code Duello was catechized in the late eighteenth century in Ireland, where dueling was considered an important part of a young gentleman's education and the engagement of a famous duelist was a matter of pride. Twenty-seven rules were adopted covering the requirements, duties and actions for every step in the process. Basically, the insulted party would make a written request for an explanation of the insult. Then, if not satisfied, the formal challenge would be issued in writing through a second. Different rules applied depending on the nature of the insult, the choice of weapons or the progression of events. However, once the parties arrived on the field of honor, an engagement of weapons was required.

Every student of American history knows of the duel between Aaron Burr and Alexander Hamilton and of the cost to the nation by the loss of Hamilton's financial leadership. Few would consider Burr an honorable man seeking satisfaction. Even though most duels did not end in death, many Americans today do not know the full cost to the nation of dueling or the extent to which dueling permeated society during the late eighteenth and early nineteenth centuries. Shortly after signing the Declaration of Independence, Georgian Button Gwinnett was killed in a duel, pistols at twelve paces. Before losing his life to Burr, Hamilton lost a son in a duel. Commodore Stephen Decatur, hero of Tripoli and the War of 1812, died

The Jackson-Dickinson duel. *From* The Life of Andrew Jackson: President of the United State, Illustrated with Numerous Cuts *by (Maine's own) Seba Smith, 1838.*

in a duel with Commodore James Barron, a man he had called a coward in performance of duty. Author of "The Star-Spangled Banner," Francis Scott Key, lost his son Daniel to a duel over, of all things, the speed of a steamboat. Revolutionary War generals Nathanael Greene and Israel Putnam; Dewitt Clinton, Sam Houston, Jim Bowie, Henry Clay and his cousin Cassius Marcellus Clay, John Randolph, Abraham Lincoln, Daniel Webster, even Mark Twain and many others were challenged or engaged in duels. By 1804, dueling was so common that the Reverend Lyman Beecher, father of Henry Ward Beecher, sermonized, "Dueling is a great sin. We are murderers. We are a nation of murderers, while we tolerate and reward the perpetrators of the crime."

The preeminent American duelist was Andrew Jackson, military hero and seventh president of the United States. He was reputedly involved in some capacity or fought in as many as 103 duels, fights or altercations, according to *The Indiscretions of Andrew Jackson*, an 1828 anti-Jackson campaign rag. Certainly Jackson was hotblooded and quick to anger. The eight years of Jackson's presidency were considered the heyday of dueling in Washington and America. When Jonathan Cilley came to the capital only a few years later, dueling was still very common.

## "A YOUNG MAN OF QUICK AND POWERFUL INTELLECT"

At age thirty-five in 1838, the year of his death, Jonathan Cilley was a young man just hitting his stride. The grandson of a Revolutionary War general and brother of a hero of the War of 1812, Cilley was born in Epping, New Hampshire, in 1802. He came to Maine to study at Bowdoin College and graduated with the famous class of 1825. Of the thirty-eight graduates, Nathaniel Hawthorne and Longfellow are the most famous today, but the others were well known in their time as politicians, authors, doctors, lawyers, clergymen and businessmen.

Cilley was a good student, graduated near the top of his class and demonstrated a keen interest in politics. He was a natural orator and a popular leader with a practical mind. Hawthorne wrote glowing praise of his friend in a sketch that was widely circulated at the time of Cilley's death. He went on at length:

The Ruggles Mansion on Main Street in Thomaston as it looks today. *David Higgins photo.*

> *In few words, let us characterize him at the outset of life as a young man of quick and powerful intellect, endowed with sagacity and tact, yet frank and free in his mode of action, ambitious of good influence, earnest, active, and persevering, with an elasticity and cheerful strength of mind which made difficulties easy, and the struggle with them a pleasure.*

Cilley had that charisma that marks a successful politician. His folksy charm made him a natural with his future constituents at all levels of society. In his sketch, Hawthorne hinted at "harsher and sterner traits" in an iron framework that would rise to the surface later in Cilley's life.

After graduation from Bowdoin, Cilley moved to Thomaston, where he clerked in the law offices of John Ruggles, a powerful Democrat. Cilley's star rose quickly. He soon established his own law office and married Deborah Prince, the daughter of a wealthy businessman. In 1832, Cilley, by then well known in Thomaston, was a prime candidate for political office and followed his old mentor, Ruggles, to Augusta. Ruggles moved into a judgeship. The two men soon fell out, leaving Cilley to wend his way through state politics not only without the guidance of the older man but also with his animosity. The cause of the problem was that Ruggles did not think he was getting the total support from Cilley that he felt was his due. The man was known to

The Cilley House on Main Street in Thomaston as it looks today. Ruggles's house can be seen through the trees to the left. *David Higgins photo.*

hold a grudge. The animosity between the two became so great that Ruggles forbade his wife and children from associating with the Cilley family who lived right next door. The two men wrangled their way through state politics for the next five years.

Even when Ruggles moved on to the U.S. Senate, his friends in the party kept the pressure on Cilley. At one point, Cilley, who was accused of perjury by the *Eastern Argus*, sued the Portland newspaper for slander and won. In 1835, he was banned from the Democratic caucuses, and an attempt was made to expel him from the party. Cilley was a popular man with a great deal of support among the younger politicians. Instead of being sent packing, Cilley rallied his support and ended up as Speaker of the Maine House. Despite opposition from the Whigs and from the Ruggles faction of his own party, he made an easy step into the U.S. House of Representatives in 1836.

Eve Anderson, the editor of Cilley's collected letters, wrote of him, "Jonathan Cilley did not make enemies because of any fault in his character; he made enemies because he was resolute in his beliefs." It was a tough time in American politics to be resolute. Although Hawthorne described Cilley as a fair man and not one to hold a grudge, it is also more than apparent that he loved the sport of politics and played to win. As a young Turk, Cilley cut a swath about Washington. He had that popularity with the common man that had become so important in politics during the presidency of Andrew

Jackson. He was not only a Democrat and a man of the people but also a professional and savvy politician to the core. It was evident when Cilley first entered the House of Representatives that he was not likely to give way or buckle under bullying from opposing forces. The threat of a challenge, the stigma of lacking courage, silenced many men or made them pick their arguments carefully. Not Cilley!

## "THINGS DO NOT GO HERE BY MERIT BUT BY PULLING STRINGS"

A confrontation was inevitable. It arose over a charge of influence peddling by a member of Congress. Matthew L. Davis of the New York *Courier and Enquirer* reported the story in his column, writing, "Things do not go here by merit but by pulling strings; make it my interest and I will pull the strings for you." Davis did not name the perpetrator who spoke these words. His editor, Colonel James Watson Webb, called for an immediate investigation by Congress and was supported on February 12, 1838, by Representative Henry Wise, a Virginia Whig, on the floor of the House. Cilley jumped right in, saying it was inappropriate for such an investigation to be launched based solely on nonspecific charges made in the press. Perhaps events would have transpired differently if Cilley did not continue his argument with an attack on Webb. Specifically, Cilley said Webb had opposed the National Bank during the Jackson administration's bank crisis but later switched sides to line his pockets with loans from the same bank. Therefore, Cilley doubted Webb's reliability in this situation. These were fighting words.

Jonathan Cilley, 1802–1838. *Library of Congress.*

Interestingly enough, the unnamed member who started this argument turned out to be Senator John Ruggles. From letters that Eve Anderson included in her *A Breach of Privilege*, on February 13, Cilley wrote to his wife, who was at home in Thomaston with the family, to read some articles in the *Globe* describing Ruggles's attempts at influence peddling regarding a lock patent that a Mr. Jones of Newark wished to sell to the U.S. Post Office according to Henry Wise. On the following day, Cilley again wrote Deborah, saying, "Ruggles gets deeper in the mire the more he struggles to get out of his scrape...He is a disgrace to our State." The charges, later investigated, proved to be a misinterpretation of events involving the unfiled patent. Ruggles never received money for some legal work he did involving the patent and was exonerated by a Senate investigation. Unfortunately, this rather trivial event put other more disastrous ones into action.

## "I DECLINED TO RECEIVE IT BECAUSE I CHOSE TO BE DRAWN INTO NO CONTROVERSY WITH HIM"

The situation festered for eight days until Webb arrived in Washington for a dinner hosted by the notable Whig Daniel Webster and attended by many high-ranking Whigs, including Henry Clay. Colonel Webb was a well-known bully who beat up rival editors on the streets. Dueling had already cost him his military career. Now Webb was bent on obtaining satisfaction. The dinner provided him with a venue and opportunity to press his attack. At first, he could not find anyone to carry his challenge, but then William Jordan Graves, a Whig representative from Kentucky, consented to carry the challenge to Cilley. Graves was in all probability acting at the direction of another more powerful Kentuckian, Henry Clay—the Great Compromiser—but certainly Graves was no stranger to the backrooms of partisan politics. The Webb affair provided an opportunity for the Whigs to embarrass the opposition. Whatever his connection or feelings on the events, Graves must have felt compelled by his superiors to act as messenger boy.

The note Graves carried demanded an explanation of Cilley's comments about Webb that were made on the floor of the House on the twelfth. Cilley refused to take the note when he was apprised of its contents and "threw it somewhat contemptuously into the hat of Mr. G." in the incident as described by Don C. Seitz in *Famous American Duels*. Graves became agitated and told Cilley that if he did not accept Webb's note, then he would be compelling

William Jordan Graves, 1805–1848. *Library of Congress.*

Graves to demand satisfaction for himself. Cilley told Graves, "I have determined not to receive the note of Colonel Webb, because I will not hold myself responsible to any conductor of the public press for words spoken in debate on this floor." Therein lies the crux of the matter.

Graves stepped away and, after some consultation with his friends (notably Henry Clay), returned demanding that Cilley provide assurances in writing that he did not base his decision to refuse Webb's note on any objections to Webb as a gentleman. In theory, if Webb were no gentleman, then neither was Graves because he carried the man's challenge. Graves would then be compelled to deliver a challenge of his own. Cilley, of course, refused to write any such thing. He had already said on the floor of the House of Representatives that Webb was no gentleman. Any such written assertion now would mean he had capitulated to the Whigs. He couched his reply as follows:

> *I declined to receive it because I chose to be drawn into no controversy with him. I neither affirmed* [n]*or denied anything in regard to his character; but when you remarked that this course on my part might place you in an unpleasant situation, I stated to you, and now repeat, that I intended by the refusal no disrespect to you.*

He would not bow to an attempt by the press to influence or control what an elected official said while conducting his duties. He would not be bullied or silenced by threats. The actions of Webb, Wise, Graves and others caused a breach of privilege of Cilley's rights and duties as an elected representative and were, as such, against the law and the Constitution. His little group of enemies was not deterred. From this point on, variations of this demand were played and replayed in conversation and writing right up to the point when Cilley was shot down.

## "IT IS AN ATTEMPT TO BROWBEAT US"

On the morning of February 23, Graves sent Wise, the Whig who had called for the original investigation in the House, to Cilley's lodgings with his own challenge. Henry Clay himself had written this new challenge, and Graves carefully copied it over. Wise kept the original written in Clay's own hand. The challenge stated that Cilley had insulted Graves's honor by implying that Graves had served the purposes of a dishonorable man. Cilley felt this new challenge was absurd but accepted rather than disgrace himself with "humiliating concessions." Embarrassment turned out to be the least of Cilley's problems.

Cilley was no fool; he knew the reasoning and the players behind the challenge. It was like a "shadowy pretext," as Hawthorne described it in his biographical sketch of his college friend, in which party politics "overstepped the imaginary distinction which…separates manslaughter from murder." Cilley stated it this way to Colonel Schaumbourg, who acted as his "friend" in the subsequent duel:

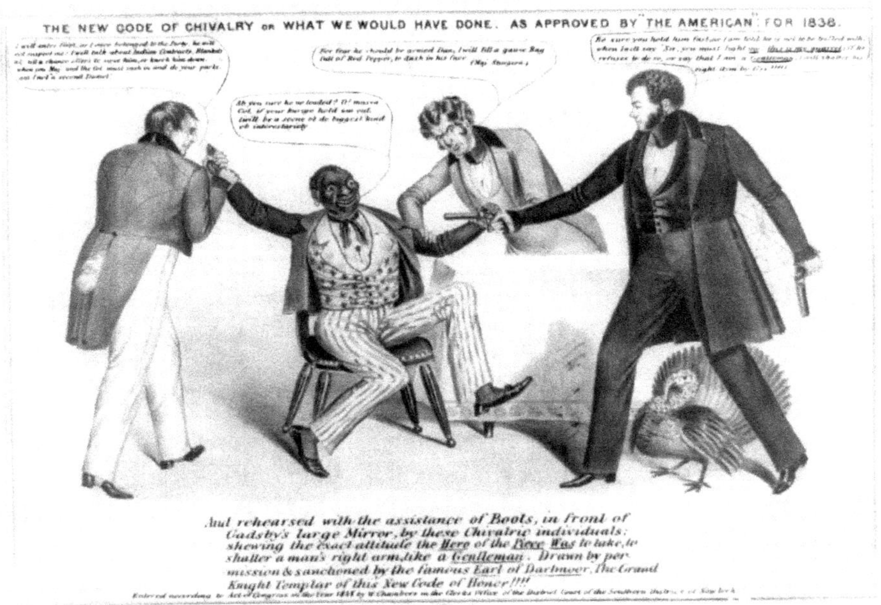


"The new code of chivalry or what we would have done…" (1838) shows James Webb conducting a practice session regarding the Cilley challenge. *Library of Congress.*

> *I see into this whole affair. Webb has come on here to challenge me because he, and perhaps others, think that, as I am from New England, I am to be bluffed, and Mr. Webb will proclaim himself a brave man, having obtained an acknowledgment on my part that he is a gentleman and a man of honor. But they have calculated without their host. Although I know that the sentiment of New England is opposed to dueling, I am sure that my people will be better pleased if I stand the test than disgrace myself by humiliating concessions. Sir, the name I bear will never permit me to cower beneath the frown of mortal man. It is an attempt to browbeat us, and because they think that (and they think that because) I am from the East I will tamely submit.*

It was a partisan attempt in a time in which partisanship was drawn up on regional lines to force the opponent to make an embarrassing retraction that could be used in the future to further discredit and intimidate him. In the game of politics, Cilley could not, would not, allow this to happen.

By terms of the code, Cilley was to choose the weapons. As remembered by General George Jones, Cilley's choice of rifles at eighty yards was because, he said, "I expect the Kentuckian would prefer pistols, therefore I demand rifles that I may be on an equality." Wise claimed later to have opposed the use of rifles but was overruled by Clay, who said that Graves was "a Kentuckian and can never back from a rifle." Neither Cilley nor Graves had ever before fought a duel, but the Whigs later claimed that Cilley was the more experienced rifleman.

So was Cilley as hotblooded as his various challengers, or was he a man who would not buckle under intimidation and who was maneuvered into an untimely and barbaric death? Certainly Cilley did not have to fight. Author Hamilton Cochran described many instances in which prominent men refused and were not thought of poorly. General Winfield Scott was once challenged by General Andrew Jackson and refused. He told Jackson to console himself with a few epithets, like coward, and wait until the next war to see if they were true. Congressman John Randolph of Virginia was challenged in 1807 by General James Wilkinson and insulted the general's honor by refusing to fight. Wilkinson was infuriated and "posted" notices around Washington declaring Randolph to be "a prevaricating, base, calumniating scoundrel, poltroon and coward." Randolph was not concerned. In the eyes of Randolph and many Americans, Wilkinson had no honor to be insulted because he was heavily implicated as an accomplice in Aaron Burr's treason trial.

If communications had been more immediate and timely, perhaps Deborah Cilley would have been able to sway her husband's resolve to finally accept the challenge. As it was, Anderson records, she received his last letters on February 28 and wrote her final letter to him on March 1, the day before word reached Thomaston of his death. Sadly, he would never read her plea. She wrote, "Ruggles wrote you have been challenged by Webber of New York. I will not believe it as it has come only from him." And further, "I will never believe you will accept a challenge is it not the same as suicide and murder horrible I will not think of it a moment." The depth of her fears and emotions shows in the total lack of punctuation and grammar.

If Cilley was truly cornered and could not avoid accepting a challenge, he might still have controlled the situation by his choice of weapons. Abraham Lincoln suggested cow dung as the appropriate choice of weapons between himself and another lawyer. An ex-whaler captain named S.M. Harvey was challenged by a Creole gentleman in New Orleans after Harvey blackened his eye during a card game. Harvey told the man's second that his choice of weapons was whale harpoons at twenty paces. He then demonstrated the use of the harpoon by splintering a tree in his backyard. The challenge was quickly dropped. Of course, choosing a weapon with a cultural advantage is the sort of thing that can backfire. Fish chum at twenty paces is one thing; peaveys on rolling logs in a surging river might not be as easy.

## "THEY MUST THIRST MIGHTILY FOR MY BLOOD"

Having met at the Anacostia Bridge sometime between 1:30 and 2:30 p.m. on February 24, 1838, the two dueling parties proceeded to Bladensburg, Maryland. Located just across the district's border, Bladensburg already had achieved a certain notoriety. Dueling was outlawed in the District of Columbia but not in Maryland; Bladensburg was just a short distance to the northeast. More than fifty duels were said to have been fought there in the first half of the nineteenth century. Enough blood was shed to name the local stream "Blood Run." Naval hero Stephen Decatur and Francis Scott Key's son Daniel both lost their lives on the field at Bladensburg. The Cilley-Graves duel was to become equally infamous.

Don Carlos Seitz, Horatio King and S.M. Watson all give complete and detailed accounts of the duel and are compiled here to describe the events.

The two duelists were attended by their seconds, General George Jones and Henry Wise. Cilley was also assisted by Representative Jesse Bynum (North Carolina), Senator and surgeon Alexander Duncan (Ohio) and dragoon Colonel H.W. Shaumbourg. Graves was attended by Dr. J.M. Folz. Congressmen John C. Calhoun and Richard Menifee (Kentucky) were either part of Graves's party or they were unofficial guests who observed the duel from a distance. The two hack drivers, the owner of the land and another unknown person were the only other observers. Henry Clay was conspicuously absent. By some accounts, he spent the day at home just sick over the situation. By others, he and John J. Crittenden set out from Washington to stop the duel. Mrs. Graves sent out the marshal of the District of Columbia to stop the duel. On the other hand, Colonel Webb, armed to the teeth, searched Washington for the duelists all the while proclaiming he and not Graves should fight Cilley. He wanted to shoot Cilley on the spot if found or at least shatter his right arm. In the end, none of these men found the location of the duel despite that site's notoriety.

Scene in Washington on Sunday, February 25, 1838, shows James Webb armed to the teeth and condemns him for Cilley's murder. *Library of Congress.*

Upon arrival at the field, the seconds worked out a few points of propriety. They marked out the snowy ground. Wise won the choice of position and chose to place his man against the tree line. This put Cilley at a disadvantage facing into the wind in the open field. Shortly after three o'clock, the two seconds oversaw the loading of the rifles, and Jones carefully instructed the principals on the terms of engagement. The principals then took up their positions with the seconds and other observers arranged along the line of fire. Because Wise won the choice of position, Jones gave the word to fire. Cilley's gun discharged into the ground either on purpose or by accident. Guns used in duels were frequently refined to have hair triggers. Graves aimed carefully but missed.

The seconds met to mediate the situation. Jones asked Wise if Graves was satisfied. The two men argued points of procedure. Wise felt that Graves's honor could be restored if Cilley would provide some explanation and disclaimer as to why, yet again, Cilley refused to accept Colonel Webb's letter from Wise's hand. He wanted the explanation in writing but would settle for a verbal explanation first. This verbal exchange proved to be a problem. Jones claimed later that he clearly stated that Cilley meant no disrespect to Graves but refused Webb's letter because he chose not to be drawn into a controversy with Webb. Graves was not part of the issue. Wise couched the explanation somewhat differently. He said the explanation was that Cilley, in declining "to receive the note from Mr. Graves, purporting to be from Colonel Webb…meant no disrespect to Mr. Graves, because he entertained for him then, as he does now, the highest respect and most kind feelings; but [he] refused to disclaim disrespect for Colonel Webb, because he does not choose to be drawn into an expression of an opinion of him." The Wise explanation makes quite different inferences.

After much conversation between all parties, Mr. Graves expressed that his honor was not restored, and a second round was required. This time, the shots were reversed. Graves fired into the ground, and Cilley missed—but just barely. The seconds again came together for a discussion that was not much different from that held after the first round. Jones said two rounds were enough to render satisfaction to Mr. Graves. Wise's explanation led more to the real crux of the matter: Colonel Webb. After all, Mr. Graves, a man of honor, would not carry the letter of a man who was not also a gentleman and man of honor, and so on. Cilley again refused to hold himself accountable for words said about Webb in the House debate. Graves told Wise, "I must have one more shot!" Cilley said to Bynum, "They must thirst mightily for my blood." The rifles were reloaded for a third round. As the seconds discussed the possibility of shortening the distance in subsequent

The old dueling grounds in Bladensburg, Maryland, taken between 1910 and 1926. *Library of Congress.*

rounds, the duelists fired. Graves was again spared; Cilley was hit. His femoral artery was severed, and he quickly bled to death. At Wise's inquiry, Jones replied, "My friend is dead, sir!"

## "God Will Plead the Cause of the Widow"

Somebody had to give the terrible news to the family. Anderson tells the story. The word did not arrive in Thomaston until March 2 and was delivered to Deborah Cilley by Reverend Washburn. The scene was heart rending. The reverend's wife, who accompanied him to the Cilley home, was so upset that she wrote an emotional letter to Graves that ended with "GOD who will plead the cause of the widow, and the Fatherless, will be your Judge also and oh, may you find mercy when you stand before his righteous Tribunal." Certainly this could not help but have an effect on Graves.

A Washington funeral was held and attended by President Van Buren, his vice president, foreign ministers and congressmen, as well as a throng of ordinary people. Notably, members of the Supreme Court refused to attend. Cilley's body was placed in the vault at the Congressional Cemetery until returned home to Maine in April. In Rockport, Cilley's pallbearers went right into those cold April waters to take up the coffin from the ship's tender and bring it ashore. Cilley was laid to rest on April 19 in Elm Grove Cemetery at Thomaston. A collection was taken up among Cilley's friends and supporters to raise a suitable monument. In 1841, for a sum of $500, a seventeen-foot-tall granite monument topped by a marble urn was placed over the grave. Today, the base remains, but the pillar and urn are not there.

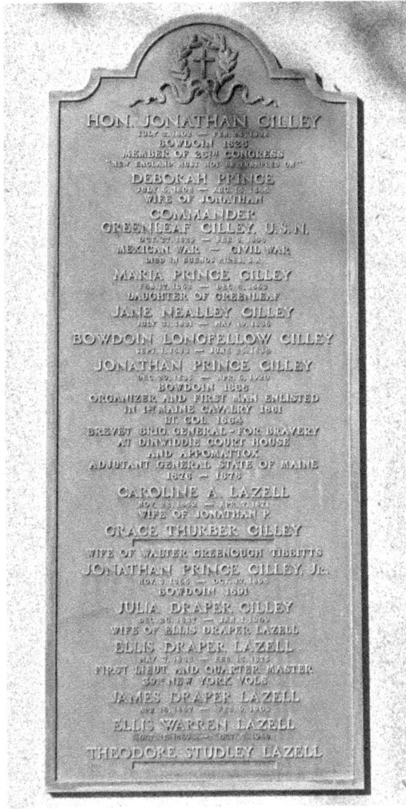


*Left*: The Cilley gravestone at the Village Cemetery in Thomaston, Maine. *David Higgins photo*. *Right*: A close-up of the inscription of the Cilley stone showing the public service of his sons and descendants. *David Higgins photo*.

## "Murder Most Foul"

But Cilley's death is not the end of the story. Public outcry was immediate. The Washington correspondent for the *New York Evening Post* wrote of his visit to Cilley's Washington boardinghouse in the evening after the duel as a "horrid and harrowing spectacle. Lying on the floor wrapped in a blanket smeared with his blood, lay the ghastly corpse of Jonathan Cilley." The reporter further editorialized by calling Cilley's death "a cold blooded and deliberate murder," saying that the Mainer "has fallen a victim to a false and bloody code in a wretched quarrel." The *Post* was also quick to point a finger at Colonel Webb, the editor of the rival *New York Courier and Enquirer*, calling him "a contemptible person." This was just the beginning, nationally, of what became a furor of debate and condemnation about this duel and about dueling in general.

In Maine, the *Argus* headline read, "Murder Most Foul." The article was quick to point out that the event was clearly based on a policy "that those who can't be intimidated must be silenced." The *Argus* article also highlighted a geographically sectarian attitude that was pervasive in the North. "A National Government which will not protect Northern members of Congress in the fearless discharge of their duty is not worth preserving...The North, depend on it, will not submit to have her representatives shot down like dogs, by the trained assassins of any section of the country." Democrats were quick to put forth the theory of conspiracy by the Whigs to rid themselves of an up-and-coming, resourceful and intelligent opponent.

Northerners were not the only ones to cry foul. Opinion, of course, split sharply along party lines. Interestingly, even former president Andrew Jackson, the dean of duelists and a westerner, spoke out against this particular duel according to Hatch. He wrote to his successor, President Martin Van Buren, "I cannot write on the murderous death of poor Chilley [*sic*]. If Congress does not do something to wash out the stain of the murdered blood of Chilley from its Walls, it will raise a flame in the public [erasure] mind against it not easily to be quelled. Chilley was sacrificed." Clearly, the Democratic Party had lost a player.

The Whigs, on the other hand, were more subtle. Whig spokesmen pointed out that many Democrats knew about the intended duel and did not move to prevent it. They claimed that Cilley's friends had great confidence in their man and expected him to win. He had, after all, purportedly put eleven rifle shots into a target the size of a man's hand only the day before the duel. The great American journalist Horace

Greeley was at the time of the duel producing a publication for the New York Whig Party. He condemned dueling as abhorrent but pointed out that both players suffered the after effects. Granted, one was dead, but some sympathy should be awarded to Graves, who must live "to execrate through years of anguish and remorse the hour when he was impelled to imbue his hands in the blood of a fellow being."

As can be expected, religious leaders condemned dueling as sinful but found Cilley as culpable as Graves and all the others involved. Reverend Maltby of Bangor preached from his pulpit, "Shame! Shame! The Congress of the United States...are honoring with a public burial, a man who died in the act of murder, setting at naught the laws of God and man." With a similar sentiment, William Farley spoke out more calmly at the Thomaston meetinghouse, "It was a fatal, an unjustifiable error."

## "A MAN WHO CAME TO THE HOUSE WITH HIS HANDS AND FACE DRIPPING WITH THE BLOOD OF MURDER"

Soon after the Washington funeral, the Maine delegation called for an investigation of the whole affair. A committee was appointed. On April 21, the seven-man committee returned its opinion. The four-man majority (three from the North) "viewed the breach of the rights and privileges of the House on the part of Mr. Graves, to have been an offense of this high character against the vital principle of deliberative assembly and of representative government." They called for Graves's expulsion and the censure of Wise and Jones. They left Webb to the "chastisement of public opinion."

A great debate rose on the floor of the House and can be read in the congressional records. The Whigs were up in arms; this was clearly an attempt by the committee to try, convict and punish the men. Ex-president and then representative John Quincy Adams called the report a greater violation of the privileges of the House than the actual events of the duel. The debate became "warm." Both Wise and Graves addressed the House, pointing out the inappropriateness of the proceeding that would allow them to be judged and condemned by "four political adversaries without a chance to speak." Graves made an affecting speech claiming never to have been involved in a duel in any capacity before. He maintained his innocence of any knowledge of a wider purpose or conspiracy. He was contrite but blamed public opinion and an honor system that trapped him in the circumstances of the event. Wise was less self-deprecating and called the committee despotic in its assumption of judicial powers. It was a great whitewashing of their bullying and inappropriate behavior. Adams denounced Wise but not Graves as the truly guilty party, calling him "a man who came to the House with his hands and face dripping with the blood of murder." Even Webb tried to distance himself from the condemnations by saying the challenge and duel were never his intent and should not have happened.

Interestingly enough, Henry Clay dodged any serious accusation or connection. Clay was known by many to be the mastermind of the conspiracy or at least the provocateur of events. The Great Compromiser was known to pull a few strings in the background of many events. In the end, the full committee report failed to gain acceptance. Dueling was prohibited in the district. Wise was censured; Graves was censured but not expelled. Even Jones was censured for his part as Cilley's second; presumably if Cilley had survived, he would have been censured as well.

The following year, 1839, Congress passed the antidueling act. The original bill introduced by Prentiss of Vermont called for a ten-year prison sentence for giving or accepting a challenge and a death sentence for any duelist who killed an opponent. Congress passed the bill but reduced the time to five years. A number of states followed suit with similar legislation. None of the laws seemed to have any particular inhibiting effect. Duelists became more secretive, and dueling flourished right up to the Civil War, when everyone soon had their fill of blood. Dueling was not uncommon even after the war and up through the turn of the century.

## WHAT BECAME OF THE PRINCIPAL PLAYERS?

Deborah Cilley died six years later; she never recovered from her husband's murder. Cilley left three living children. Cilley's oldest son, Greenleaf, was appointed a midshipman in the U.S. Navy in 1841; he was not quite twelve years old. He served in the Mexican and Civil Wars. Greenleaf married a Uruguayan woman, and interestingly enough, they were at Ford's Theater the night Lincoln was assassinated. Retiring from the navy in 1865 as a commander, Greenleaf spent much of his life in South America and died in 1899. Cilley's second son and namesake, Jonathan Prince Cilley, was born in 1835 and followed in his father's footsteps to Bowdoin and then into law practice in Thomaston. He was the first man to enlist in the First Maine

Cavalry and was reputedly as ardent an opponent as his father. After the war, he returned to Thomaston, practiced law and held many political positions. The third child, Julia Draper Cilley, was born after Cilley went to Washington in 1837; he never saw her. She married Ellis Draper Lazell, who died in 1875, leaving her with three young sons. She resided in the Cilley home in Thomaston with her brother Jonathan and their families.

The Ruggles stone in the Village Cemetery. In death, the Ruggles and Cilly are not next-door neighbors but rest more than one hundred yards apart. *David Higgins photo.*

Judge Ruggles served in the U.S. Senate from 1835 to 1841. He was chairman of the Committee of Patents and Patent Office and is known today as the "Father of the U.S. Patent Office." He was himself an inventor and holds U.S. Patent 1 for a special type of train wheel. Ruggles was not reelected after the Cilley duel but returned to his Thomaston law office.

William Graves served out his term of office but did not run for reelection in 1840. Instead, he returned to his law practice in Kentucky and died ten years after the duel. Whether he found mercy when he stood before God's "righteous tribunal," as suggested by Reverend Washburn's wife, is unknown.

In the years just before and after the Graves-Cilley affair, Wise himself was a principal in duels with two southern congressmen. Henry Wise continued in politics, served as minister to Brazil under President Tyler, governor of Virginia just before the Civil War and a general in the Confederate army. Near the end of the Civil War, General Wise was bested on the battlefield by General Jonathan P. Cilley. After the war, he returned to his law practice in Richmond, Virginia.

Interestingly enough, Colonel Webb was the only person ever convicted under New York's antidueling law. In 1842, he was convicted of fighting a duel with Representative Thomas Marshall of Kentucky, who was in disagreement with Henry Clay over banking and the annexation of Texas. Webb printed some derogatory articles in the *Courier*; certainly there is a trend here. Marshall challenged him and, in a duel in Kentucky, shot Webb in the knee, crippling him for life. Webb was sentenced to two years in Sing Sing but was pardoned after a few days by Governor William H. Seward. So much for censure and public opinion! Seward initially ran against Lincoln for the Republican presidential nomination of 1860 (over which he and Webb fell out) and later served as Lincoln's secretary of state. These two politicians spent considerable effort trying to find a political appointment for Webb that would keep him out of the way. Turkey was offered, but Webb held out and finally accepted an appointment as U.S. ambassador to Brazil. Between 1827 and 1861, when he sold the *Courier*, Webb used the newspaper first in support of the Democratic Party and then as a Whig mouthpiece. The paper, like its owner, was vicious, racist and anti-abolitionist.

Although the Cilley-Graves duel can hardly be considered a cause of the Civil War, it certainly has its place in the events leading up to the war. It really had nothing to do with the abolition of slavery, economics or states' rights, but it had everything to do with the partisanship that was destroying the relations between the states. It remains a good example of how quickly animosity can build and explode in small sidelines when the bigger issues are causing so much dissention.

# 6

# Jefferson Davis's Last Respite

Many of us in the North and in Maine remember Jefferson Davis solely as the first and only president of the Confederacy. Our position on the other side during the Civil War places him strongly in the enemy camp and perhaps doesn't lead us to study the facts about his life very dispassionately. Few of us could tell much about his other life before the Confederacy even though only three years before his presidency he spent a summer in Maine and was quite a celebrity.

## "The Hero of Buena Vista"

The early life of Jefferson Finis Davis, born in Kentucky in 1808, seems like the stuff from which legend is made. He was named for the third president of a country that his father fought to free and was born in the West like many of the leaders of the coming generation. Davis was even born in a log house not unlike his future adversary Abraham Lincoln, but with these differences: his house had glass windows, his father's farm was worked by slaves and young Jefferson was educated in private schools. The family soon moved to Mississippi, where Davis lived most of his nonpublic life as a planter.

A family military history that included not only his father's Revolutionary War service but also that of three older brothers, who served in the War of 1812, might have been enough to influence young Jefferson Davis to pursue

A lithographic portrait of Jefferson Davis published by Currier & Ives between 1856 and 1907. *Library of Congress.*

a military career; certainly a childhood visit with the hero of New Orleans, Andrew Jackson, was auspicious. Davis attended West Point, graduating in 1828 neither at the top nor the bottom of his class. His military career began with service during the 1832 Black Hawk War. According to biographer Hudson Strode, ten years later during the Mexican War, "Davis won a fame second only to General Taylor" for his strategy and leadership at Buena Vista that trapped Santa Anna's troops in a devastating cross fire. He ended the day with a boot full of blood and a foot shattered by pieces of brass spur. Returning home to his plantation, Davis was invalided for some time, enduring not only a great deal of pain but also a media blitz that painted him as the "Hero of Buena Vista." He declined President Polk's (unsolicited) commission as brigadier general but, in mid-1847, accepted a commission to fill a vacancy in the U.S. Senate.

## "To Go Out of the Union, with the Constitution, Rather Than Abandon the Constitution, to Remain in an Union"

Davis was predictably, geographically and economically a Democrat, a slave owner and a southerner. Slavery was, he felt, necessary to a healthy southern and perhaps even world economy. In return for servitude, slave owners were obligated to protect, guide and slowly raise their slaves into a suitable place in the (white) world, where they certainly would never be the equals of their masters. Davis felt that emancipation was something the slaves would not be ready for in his lifetime. Throughout his early political career, Davis followed a definite and quite predictable political path that allowed slavery and, especially, promoted states rights' through a strict interpretation of the Constitution. States' rights were the true cornerstone of his political philosophy.

Davis was considered a disciple of the South Carolinian firebrand John C. Calhoun. He rejected any notion of restricting slavery, opposed the Compromise of 1850 and felt that the Fugitive Slave Acts were unenforceable in the northern climate because of the overt activities of the radical abolitionists. After Calhoun's death in 1850, Davis continued to be relentless in demanding protection of the South's rights under the Constitution. As for secession, Davis made it quite clear in an 1850 edition of the *Mississippi Free Trader* that he had never supported secession or a dissolution of the Union but felt that the South should be prepared "to go out of the Union, with the Constitution, rather than abandon the Constitution, to remain in an Union."

Disillusioned by Washington politics, Davis left the city in 1851. He returned in 1853 when newly elected president Franklin Pierce, a New Hampshire Democratic and Bowdoin graduate, brought him back from his plantation retirement to serve as secretary of war. In this position, Davis did much to build up the strength and efficiency of the army that the Confederacy would soon oppose. One such project was the construction of Fort Gorges in Portland Harbor.

After the Pierce administration, Jefferson Davis returned to the Senate, where he was considered the best southern speaker/spokesman of the time. Horace Greeley, antislavery editor of the *New York Tribune*, described Jefferson Davis at this time as

> *unquestionably the foremost man of the South today. Every Northern Senator will admit that from the Southern side of the floor the most formidable to meet in debate is the thin, polished, intellectual-looking Mississippian with the impassioned demeanor, the habitual courtesy and the occasional unintentional arrogance...He belongs to a higher grade of public men in whom formerly the slave-holding democracy was prolific.*

As spokesman for the South, Jefferson Davis was in demand to speak almost constantly on the floor of the Senate and at political and social events. It was an increasingly frantic pace that he could not sustain.

## "I Do Not See Why This Eye Has Not Burst"

Varina Davis in a full-length carte de visite portrait taken sometime between 1860 and 1870. *Library of Congress.*

During the winter of 1858, Jefferson Davis, who had suffered serious health problems (including malaria) in the past, became very sick. Stress and the heavy speaking load were attributed to bringing on this almost fatal illness. In fact, his speaking load was so intense that he suffered facial paralysis. By the end of February, Davis was so seriously rundown that he caught a cold that turned into laryngitis and then neuralgia of the left side of his face and badly inflamed his left eye. He lay for weeks in a darkened room unable to speak or see. His left eye was actually so painfully swollen that his own doctor thought it would burst.

Varina Davis, his second wife, nursed her husband relentlessly; Davis later attributed her care with saving his vision and probably his life. This was a difficult time; she had two young children of her own, plus her much younger brother and her husband's namesake, "Jeffy" Davis Howell, who was in her care. Jeffy became seriously ill with scarlet fever. She nursed little Jeffy upstairs in the same house where she also desperately tended her husband downstairs. For the family, it was a terrible time. It is a tribute to Jefferson Davis that a large number and variety of men sat by his sick bed; these not only included all manner of southerners but also Lord Napier, a British diplomat, and William Seward and Charles Sumner from the northern opposition. These men not only kept him company but also read aloud to him and wrote for him.

## "To a Higher Latitude for a Month or Two, After the Adjournment of Congress"

Later in the spring, Davis, much emaciated, began to return to the Senate for at least an hour each day. His physician prescribed a sea voyage or a trip to a northerly cooler climate to improve his appetite and speed his slow recovery. When Congress adjourned, the Davis family thought to visit friends, particularly former president Franklin Pierce, in Europe, but this seemed too much for a man in Davis's weakened condition. Instead the family chose—Maine? Why would this consummate southerner choose to visit the bastion of his opposition, New England, at a time when sectional strife had risen to such a state of distress?

Historians have hypothesized that, in his trip through the North, Davis wished to scout out the true feelings and opinions of the opposition. Perhaps he was even planning to run for the presidency in the next election and needed to scope out support. This seems a bit calculating for a man so recently pulled back from the grave, but as a bonus, this information gathering would not be out of the question during a recuperative vacation. In a letter to Franklin Pierce, Strode says, Davis made it clear that he could not risk a return to his Mississippi home that summer for fear of exposure to malaria. Perhaps Davis was just following orders from his physicians by going "to a higher latitude for a month or two, after the adjournment of Congress."

Davis planned to spend time with a wide range of friends during his vacation trip. Today, the decade before the Civil War is viewed as markedly black and white, North and South, but this is far from the truth. Despite the fact that the North and the South were on divergent paths, Davis had many friends in the North, including Democrats and others who were sympathetic to his views regarding states' rights. Many of his northern countrymen remembered him for his military adventures, and Jefferson Davis continued to hold their respect with his courtly demeanor and impassioned defense of the South. One particular friend, Alexander Dallas Bache, may have led the Davis family to finalize the location of their vacation to Maine. Bache, the great-grandson of Benjamin Franklin, was engaged in scientific experiments for the U.S. Coastal Survey down east in Maine that summer. In fact, it was their fast friendship from West Point days that first got Jefferson Davis up out of his sickbed earlier that spring. Davis returned to the Senate above the objections of his wife and doctor to address the body on an appropriation for the survey, saying, according to Strode, "I must go if it kills me. It is good for the country and good for the friend of my youth."

## "The Medium Through Which Maine Tenders an Expression of Regard to Her Sister Mississippi"

The Davises decided to travel by sea for his health. The family left Baltimore on the *Joseph Whitney* at the end of June with their daughter Maggie and baby son, Jeff Jr., but apparently not the little brother-in-law Jeffy. They put in at Boston and then traveled by packet to Portland. The voyage, just as the doctor predicted, did much to improve the southern statesman's health. Davis was soon able to leave the eye uncovered except in bright sunlight, his spirits lifted and he began to socialize with his fellow passengers. The sea air and a little vacation with the family were having the desired effects.

Socially, the Davis family found travel in the North quite agreeable as well. Jefferson Davis was a famous man, and he was treated with politeness and respect for his position and his opinion as well as his person. On the Fourth of July, while on board the *Joseph Whitney*, he was prevailed upon by Captain S. Howes to make a little speech; Davis was, after all, a distinguished senator. In this first vacation speech, however informal, Davis called for peace, Union and the Constitution. He said:

> *Trifling politicians in the South, or in the North, or in the West, may continue to talk otherwise, but it will be to no avail...the good sense and the good feeling of the people had thus far averted any catastrophe destructive of our Constitution and the Union. It was fraternity and an elevation of principle which rose superior to sectional or individual aggrandizement that the foundations of our Union were laid.*

This rousing but fraternal speech set a pattern for others during his travels around Maine during the remainder of the summer. Most of Davis's speeches can be found online at Project Gutenburg.

The Davis family was quite taken with Portland and its beautiful harbor. The northern climate and the sea breezes continued to work a cure on Davis's health. The family stayed at Mrs. Blanchard's boardinghouse, where on July 9, four nights after their arrival, they were serenaded by the locals. The southerners were charmed. Afterward, Davis stood on the front steps and gave an impromptu speech. Perhaps he was surprised not to be vilified as a slave owner. He was, he said, pleased to be "the medium through which Maine tenders an expression of regard to her sister Mississippi." He plugged one of his pet projects, the Transcontinental Railroad, as a unifying endeavor. Again Davis condemned sectionalism and commended a national

A lithograph made from a drawing by Esteria Butler of the west view of the campus of Bowdoin College between 1836 and 1839. *Library of Congress.*

spirit that would keep the country whole. As a senator, he said, he was under obligation to the whole country, and indeed, he must have felt the goodwill and possibility of his own words in this northern city. Portlanders were likewise charmed with the southern gentleman and his family. For the next month, they threw clambakes in his honor and sailed the family out to the islands for "basket parties" or picnics.

During the first week of August, Davis ventured along the midcoast to Brunswick, where he was invited to Bowdoin's weeklong graduation celebration. There, on August 5, mere yards from the house in which Harriet Beecher Stowe wrote that seminal cause of the Civil War, *Uncle Tom's Cabin*, Bowdoin conferred upon Davis an honorary doctor of laws degree. A second honorary LLD was awarded to Maine's senator William Pitt Fessenden. An interesting set of comparisons can be made: both were U.S. senators, tall, thin and intellectual; one was from Maine and one from the South; one Republican and the other a Democrat; and, of course, one was an abolitionist and the other a slave owner. Reportedly, the two got along famously.

In general, the press loved it, but the *Portland Advertiser*, a Republican newspaper, took the opportunity to complain about the honors awarded Davis. The paper called it a "prostitution of the honors." How could the state's most prestigious college confer a degree on "an enemy to the Union?" The *Advertiser* would have preferred that Bowdoin honor a more appropriate personage; it even had a bipartisan candidate in mind: Maine's own Judge Nathan Clifford, a Democrat. There was a small flurry in the Maine media as the *Argus*, now a Democratic paper, took up the defense. Bowdoin seems to have ignored the matter, but two years later, in 1860, when enough time had passed, Clifford was honored at the Bowdoin graduation with his own degree.

## "THIS BLESSED VISIT...WAS THE LAST RESPITE OF PERFECT PEACE JEFFERSON DAVIS WAS TO KNOW UNTIL HIS TWILIGHT YEARS AT BEAUVOIR ON THE GULF SHORE"

The high point of the Davis family's Maine vacation was their visit to Dallas Bache's summer survey camps in Hancock and Washington Counties. This was the second time they had made such a summer pilgrimage with Bache; the first time was a few years prior in the White Mountains of New Hampshire. The work of the U.S. Coast Survey was highly exacting and would result in very accurate distances and measurements of the countryside as well as positioning of places on the map. This kind of work was becoming critically important in the modern world of the nineteenth century economically, militarily and scientifically. Thus scientists and engineers, like Bache, were willing to exert tremendous brain power and effort to inventing mapping solutions while businessmen, leaders and politicians, like Davis, were willing to pay for these solutions.

The U.S. Coast Survey, as explained by Albert E. Theberge in his history *The Coast Survey, 1806–1867,* began early in the century under the leadership of Swiss-born Ferdinand Hassler. His theory was based on a string of six large triangles stretching between Alabama and downeast Maine. Mathematically, if the measurements of two of the angles and one of the sides (the baseline) of a triangle are known, then the third angle and the lengths of the remaining two sides can be easily determined. Each of the six primary triangles was itself made up of smaller triangles; thus, the survey method is known as triangulation. The system of smaller and smaller triangles made measurement and positioning increasingly easier and more accurate. The end result would plot every location in the country within a network of triangles. Bache took over operation of the U.S. Coast Survey in 1845 and organized the surveys into nine East and Gulf

Alexander Dallas Bache was a lifelong educator, author and incorporator of the Smithsonian, as well as superintendent of the U.S. Coast Survey. *NOAA.*

Coast units and eventually added two more survey units on the West Coast. This was a huge undertaking. His teams did meteorological and magnetic observations as well as triangulation, topography and hydrography. Bache was methodical, systematic and exacting in his scientific methods; he also promoted the political and social responsibilities and roles of science.

In August, the Davis family set out to join Bache at his survey camp in eastern Maine. They traveled by rail to Bangor and, in what was a two-day trip, proceeded east by stagecoach and spent a night at an inn on Shoppe Hill in Aurora. Throughout this portion of their Maine vacation, Varina Davis was charmed by the natural landscape and wonders from Maine's glacial past. Much later, she wrote in her memoir of her husband and their life together about the trip across a glacial esker:

> *We drove nine miles over a most wonderful natural road, called by the country people "horseback," elevated over sixty feet and sloping steeply down on each side to the valley which it intersected, like a levee built by Titans. Interspersed throughout the rich valley on either side, in the lush green grass, were the most enormous bowlders of granite, many of which looked like Egyptians tombs. As there was no stone of the kind underlying the soil, Professor Bache thought they had been left there by some great flood.*

The Davis party then journeyed by ox-drawn sled up a substantial supply road built by survey engineers to the summit of Humpback Mountain.

An invitation to join Bache on his summer survey was hardly an invitation to live rough in the wild kingdom. It was, rather, an invitation to join a civilized and quite gentrified safari and to engage in highly technical and scientific experimentation. As Professor Fairman Rogers, then the treasurer of the National Academy of Sciences, later described:

> *Bright reminiscences are those of these mountain camps, with the morning's writing, the midday dinner, the genial face of the hostess, the pleasant chat over the bottle of Rhine wine, and, if there was no observing in the afternoon, the long rambles down the hill, with the climb back again, the camp being of necessity near to the summit, finishing up with an evening of conversation or reading, unless the stars were good enough to allow themselves to be observed.*

Varina Davis, in her memoir, described the camp on Humpback Mountain as follows:

> *White tents pitched one for each of us, an excellent cook, tenderloin steaks from Bangor, vegetables from the neighboring farms, and to all this comfort was added the newest books, and an exquisite and very large musical box which played "Ah, cher la morte," and many other gems of the then new operas of Verdi. Professor Bache, who could not sing a tune, kept up a pleased murmur of musical accompaniment as an expression of his delight.*

Mount Pleasant, Mount Blue, Mount Harris, Humpback, Agamenticus, Mount Independence, Ragged Mountain and Cadillac were all used for primary triangulation in Maine, although the heliotropes raised on their summits sometimes required extension towers to reach a visible height. As Mrs. Davis later recalled, "As the sun went down and shone upon the heliotropes, one fixed star after another gleamed out on the distant hill-tops, and our heliotrope answered back again to the dumb messages sent by scientists on every hill."

Down on the Epping Plains, the baseline was chosen and surveyed in the summer of 1857 by Bache and constructed as an actual road by local farmers across the barrens in an absolutely straight line between Columbia and Deblois. It was 5.4 miles long and 25 feet wide, Theberge says, graded and leveled as much as possible. In some areas, the earth needed to be cut away, and in others, it was built up by use of stone cribs. But a relief of 140 feet and rocky soil precluded building an absolutely level baseline. Despite

An 1857 view of the graded road made to measure Epping Plains Base Line. *NOAA Central Library*.

problems with the terrain, the survey crew made remarkable progress during the following summer, 1858, measuring and marking the line with granite posts. The surveyors used 6-foot iron bars encased in a long, tin tube and supported by trestles to make their measurements. This apparatus inched along the baseline by setting the trestles in advance, placing the tube over a mark and aligning it for the measurement and then transferring the tube forward to the next trestles for the next measurements. Photographs of the Epping Plains baseline operations were the first ever made to record survey field operations. The actual photos have since been lost; however, drawings were made from the plates.

It was not unusual for Bache and other male visitors to take their wives and families along. Nor was it unusual for women visitors to receive scientific instruction from Bache along with the men or engage in taking readings and measurements. In a hitherto unheard of act, Bache employed the nineteenth-century astronomer Maria Mitchell to conduct field observations with his survey party at Mount Independence, Maine, in the summer of 1845. By the mid-1850s, he employed a number of women in the U.S. Coast Survey. During the summer of 1858, Varina Davis would have the opportunity to experience an equality of learning that few women of her century would

Bache, guests and the Coast Survey party shown using Bache's compensating apparatus to measure the Epping Plains Base Line in 1857. *NOAA Central Library*.

have. She wrote, "He read aloud at night, and a part of the day we watched him taking observations and enjoyed his clear explanations of his method." There was ample opportunity for the edification of guests; Bache was not an idle host. Theberge records that, during this summer, Bache "measured angles between 6 primary points, 8 secondary points, and an azimuth marker. In the course of this work over 1,200 horizontal angles and 500 vertical angles were measured and recorded, astronomical observations for latitude, azimuth, and time were made, as were magnetic and meteorological observations." All of this was done with no calculators and no computers.

The summer work observed by the Davis family in 1858 was just the beginning; it would take two more years of work to tie the Epping Plains Base Line to the primary triangulation. Subsequent work would require the construction of two forty-foot tripods, scaffolding and windscreens at opposite ends of the baseline. The winds were a problem, and the canvas screens prevented equipment on the nine-foot-wide platforms at the top from swaying. The end result of the arc of primary triangulation from the Providence Base Line to the Epping Plains Base Line was highly accurate, within three-tenths of an inch of closure or an accuracy of better than one part in a million. Epping Plains established Bache's reputation as a scientist extraordinaire.

According to Davis biographer Hudson Strode, "This blessed visit…was the last respite of perfect peace Jefferson Davis was to know until his twilight years at Beauvoir on the Gulf shore." Davis was able to effect a full recovery from his illness of the previous spring in the peace and solitude of the Maine woods. Remarkably, even the bugs cut him a break. Varina Davis commented on the lack of insect noise to which southerners were accustomed, saying, "The fall of a leaf could be plainly heard, and it seemed to afford relief to Mr. Davis's exacerbated nerves, after the noise and bustle of Washington, to stay in this secluded place where he could be a lotus eater for a while." As a woman who very nearly lost her husband to a devastating disease only months before, Varina Davis must have been overcome by relief. Now she wrote that they spent their time almost frivolously looking "for numerous signs of the glacial period, reasoned and wondered over them, picked up 'ghost flowers' and found exquisite mosses, sometimes a foot deep, of velvety green. Mr. Davis took our little girl with us on his shoulder, and did all the things so joyful to towns-people on an outing in the country. So health came back to his wasted form."

The Honorable Isaac Reed, Died Sept. 19th. 1882 Aet. 78 yrs.

Isaac Reed, banker, shipbuilder and "boss" of Waldoboro, Maine. *Waldoboro Historical Society*.

Folk history has it that Davis traveled about Washington County with the survey crew and by himself. Reportedly, he stayed in Cherryfield and even Deblois, as well as Aurora. Maybe all these places have a claim to a sign saying "Jeff Davis Slept Here." There's even a story that the southerner left a trunk at the inn at Schoppe Hill and told the people there to turn it over only to someone who knew his secret password. Why the subterfuge? Who knows? But it makes a good story! Among his side trips, Davis made several trips into Bangor to speak and hired a local carriage and driver to take him there.

The Davis family returned to Portland late in the month, where

Davis spoke yet again, this time at the Democratic Convention on August 24. There, he assured Maine Democrats that "there still lives a National Party, struggling and resolved bravely to struggle for the maintenance of the Constitution, the abatement of sectional hostility, and the preservation of the fraternal compact made by the Fathers of the Republic." Then he was off again on a trip down east. As a distinguished war hero, he was invited to review the militia troops at the Belfast Encampment, where he made two speeches: one on the muster field and one at a banquet that evening, both driving home his now usual message but, this time, with a martial theme.

## A VISIT WITH THE "PLUG UGLY STRAIGHT WHIG HUNKER JUNTO"

Late in August, perhaps on his Belfast trip, Davis visited Waldoboro, a town held firmly in hand by Isaac Reed and his political machine, wrote Waldoboro historian Jasper Stahl. There was political bounty to be reaped and favors to be garnered; Reed negotiated a federal customs house for Waldoboro that was probably not undeserved given the amount of shipping Waldoboro produced, but then he sold his apple orchard to the federal government as a site for that building for a nifty price. His crony John H. Kennedy became the collector of customs in Waldoboro, a plum job in the time of the town's heyday of shipbuilding and shipping.

For many years, Reed was a leading Whig in the town and the state and served in the U.S. House of Representatives in 1852–53. He left the all but dead party in 1856 to support Democrat James Buchanan's successful bid for the presidency over Republican John Fremont. Isaac Reed, a man quite capable of flattery, persuasion and virulent partisanship, could not abide the Republican Party and promised the voters in his district would vote Democratic because, he said quite flatly, "I own them." With this election, Reed began to wield his considerable power for the Democratic Party, a move that led to the Waldoboro area becoming a center for copperhead sentiment during the coming war. Reed's political machinations brought him some bad press from the *Thomaston Journal*, which managed to string a bunch of vitriolic slurs together to describe his political machinations as "the Plug Ugly Straight Whig Hunker Junto," linking them to a nineteenth-century street gang with Democratic Party aspirations and splinter groups of the Whig and Democratic Parties that were both anti-abolitionists and supporters of

The Waldoboro Customs House and Post Office built on the site of Isaac Reed's apple orchard. *David Higgins photo.*

The home of lawyer and Collector of Customs John Kennedy on the Friendship Road in Waldoboro, Maine. *David Higgins photo.*

slavery in the South. For political reasons, and not just because Reed might have been an old acquaintance from Congress, it was not surprising that Jefferson Davis would visit the town during his Maine vacation.

During his visit to Reed's stronghold, Davis was wined and dined by the local citizenry. He spent time out on the Friendship Road at Customs Collector Kennedy's big brick house and was conveyed about town in the man's new chaise. Kennedy's various political offices, his law practice and his investments (largely in southern cotton) were all quite lucrative.

The highlight of the Davis visit to Waldoboro was a dinner given in his honor at Isaac Reed's house on the site of what is now the Waldo Theater. Late that evening, a disaster almost changed the course of the Civil War and the Confederacy. After the meal and after the ladies retired, the gentlemen settled in with their cigars and their drinks for a little friendly conversation. Talk was almost certainly dominated by politics, and an agreeable time was had largely because their politics were also quite agreeable. Much wine was consumed, and the hour became quite late. Finally, Davis arose to make his exit in what can be best imagined as comic opera fashion. He bowed his way backward to the door of the dining room. There were, however, two doors side by side in the south wall of the Reed dining room: one leading to the

The Reed Mansion on Main Street in Waldoboro from an old postcard. *Waldoboro Historical Society*.

front hall and the other to the cellar. Davis was a guest who not only did not know his host's house but also was quite impaired by his host's liquor. He grabbed the wrong doorknob and, bowing, backed into the cellar doorway. Reed, a good host, snatched his guest to safety just as Davis lost his balance. Thus (according to local tradition handed down by Mary Clark to author Jasper Stahl), Isaac Reed saved Jefferson Davis from an untimely death so that he could go on to become the Confederacy's only president. Believe it or not, this is the story remembered in Waldoboro.

## "A MOST WINNING AMBASSADOR OF GOOD WILL FROM THE SOUTH"

Perhaps the capstone speech of his summer vacation was in Augusta on September 29, 1858. Davis summed up his Maine vacation experience with a knowledgeable and laudatory speech at the Augusta State Fair. He began with, "I have everywhere met courtesy and considerate attention from the hour I landed on your coast to the present time." For a man who had come to Maine fully expecting to experience prejudice brought on by sectionalism, Davis truly appreciated the Maine people and was profoundly grateful for the way Mainers treated him and his family. Strode felt that Davis seemed to fully believe and expect that Mainers treated everyone with a "sentiment which would cause you to recognize every American citizen as a brother." Davis had been toured, serenaded and wined and dined for the better part of the summer by all manner of Mainers around the state who wanted to strut their stuff before the famous man. He was obviously impressed with what he had seen during his travels about the state, and he spoke knowledgeably about Maine's timber, industries, agriculture, weather and schools. Davis spoke warmly of a very pleasant, hospitable and recuperative vacation, and in general, Maine was quite charmed by the well-spoken and cultivated southerner.

Over and over throughout the summer and again at Augusta, Davis hammered his message home. He spoke familiarly of American history and domestic and foreign affairs. He spoke with great admiration of the Constitution and the American political process. Despite a national foreboding, Davis said optimistically at Augusta, "If shadows float over our disc and threaten eclipse; if there be those who would not avert, but desire to precipitate catastrophe to the Union, these are not the sentiments of the American heart; they are rather the exceptions and should not disturb our confidence in the deep-seated sentiment of nationality." Carefully, always, Davis painted himself the honorable patriot rising above partisan sectionalism: "The whole confederacy is my country, and to the innermost fibres of my heart I love it all, and every part. I could not if I would, and would not if I could dwarf myself to mere sectionality." Mainers heard this message and recognized in Jefferson Davis "a most winning ambassador of good will from the South." Too bad nobody could bank on the coinage of this goodwill trip in the coming bad years.

## A "Propagandist for Disunion" Gets Caught "Praising the Yankees"

Well-rested, the Davis family returned south through Boston, where Davis spoke before Democrats at Faneuil Hall. During the next leg of his homeward journey, Davis spoke at the Palace Garden in New York City. Although he expected to be castigated by abolitionists over slavery, he was quite surprised instead to be taken to task for promulgating disunion, an action he claimed not to condone except as the very last resort. In November, when he returned to his home in Mississippi, he found himself facing equally disconcerting accusations of pandering to the North during his summer travels. In defense, he explained, "Was it expected that to public and private manifestations of kindness by the people of Maine, I should repel their generous approaches with epithets of abuse?" And so Jefferson Davis's Maine vacation was over, and he was thrown back into the thick of the battle for the Union.

We know what happened to Jefferson Davis, but what happened to the others in our little story?

By the end of his life, Dallas Bache had achieved fame in a number of fields, including education, science and engineering. He was one of the original founders of the Smithsonian and served on its board of managers until his death. Bache was president of the American Philosophical Society, the American Philosophical Association for the Advancement of Science and the National Academy of Sciences, as well as the author of numerous scientific papers. Certainly he was one of the top scientists of his day. Bache also served the Union during the war as vice-president of the United Sanitary Commission. Although many friendships and families were divided by our Civil War, one cannot help but speculate on the effects placed on the Bache and Davis friendship. Bache died in February 1867, not too long after the war, which did not leave the two men much opportunity to renew their friendship.

Dallas Bache's Coastal Survey became an important source of information and data during the Civil War. Surveys of the coast, completed as far south as the Carolinas, were undoubtedly used for military and naval blockade strategy. In 1863, as chief engineer in charge of the defense of Philadelphia, Bache himself used survey data for planning city defenses. The work of the survey went on during the second half of the nineteenth century, mapping both the coastal regions and the interior of the United States. The U.S. Coast Survey is still with us today under the title National Oceanic and Atmospheric Administration (NOAA).

Humpback Mountain, where the Davises visited Bache, is now known as Lead Mountain. The road the Davis family climbed in an ox-drawn sled is known locally as the Jeff Davis Road or, as Theberge dubbed it, "the Jefferson Davis Highway." It must be the only road named for the Confederate president outside the South. The Horseback is part of the same esker system as the Whaleback and remains just as Varina Davis described. Travelers today can find a similar experience by driving across the top of the Whaleback and down to Calais on the renowned "Airline," or Route 9. The baseline up on Epping Plains also remains visible today. In fact, it is the last of the baselines on the East Coast to remain visible, although it is somewhat overgrown in spots. Some of the granite intermediary markers are still visible, as are the marble markers at each end of the road. The west end marker has reportedly been vandalized.

Isaac Reed's associations with Davis in the summer of 1858 spurred him on to a closer association with conservative southern Democrats. According to Stahl, his political machine became its strongest, most partisan and ruthless in the remaining years before the Civil War. (In Reed's defense, it should be stated that between 1830 and 1860, politics across the state were particularly vicious and partisan; Reed was just highly adept in using these methods.) In the 1860 presidential election, Abraham Lincoln received only 227 votes while 347 votes were cast for the Democratic candidates (Stephen Douglas 171, John Breckinridge 95 and John Bell 81). Breckinridge was the candidate of the Deep South! Such a turnout was unheard of in the rest of Maine and shows the strength of the copperheads in Waldoboro. Reed's power and ambition declined with the passage of the Civil War, though he lived on until 1882. He was more benign in his later years, and instead of

The Waldo Theater, on the site of the Reed Mansion, with the customs house to the left. *David Higgins photo.*

political scheming, he spent his evenings, Stahl said, more humbly with "his pitcher of cider, his pan of popcorn and his dish of apples."

Reed's crony, Customs Collector John Kennedy, found his prestige and wealth were severely impacted by the war. With the South under blockade, Kennedy's cotton investments went sour, and he lost heavily. When wartime difficulties arose between the town's copperhead aristocracy and the more patriotic locals, Kennedy again paid the piper. The very same chaise

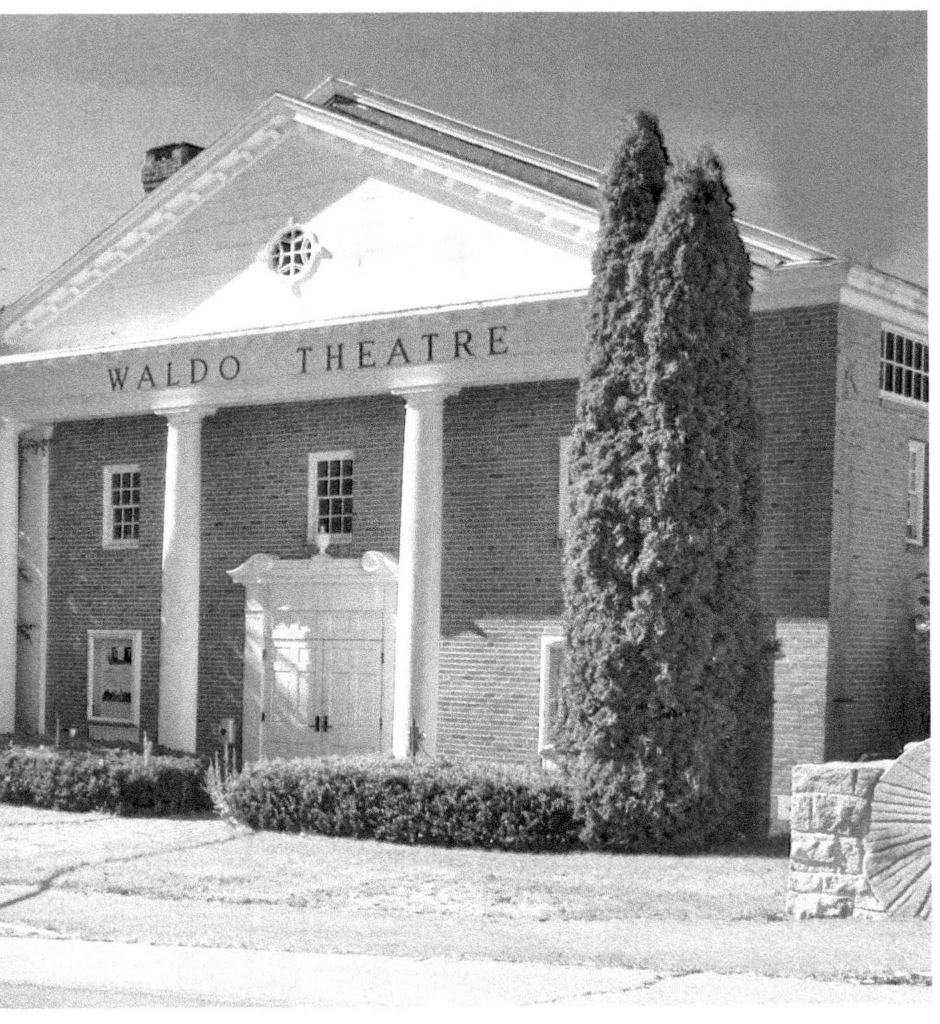


Kennedy used in the summer of 1858 was pulled out of his barn in 1862 and publicly burned by Company A of the Twenty-first Maine, which certainly remembered the special guest Kennedy so proudly drove about town a few years earlier. A few short months later, in March 1863, John Kennedy, as Stahl described him, was having trouble sleeping and took a powder from which he never awoke.

Bowdoin graciously did not retract the honorary degree it awarded to Davis. In 1889, the college received a thank-you note from Jefferson Davis to that effect. While he was at it, Davis also wrote to his hired stagecoach driver,

*Above*: The Reed family plot just inside the gate of the Waldoboro Village Cemetery off Main Street. Isaac's stone is in the center. *David Higgins photo.*

*Left*: John Kennedy's grave is at the top of the hill in the far corner of the Waldoboro Village Cemetery. *David Higgins photo.*

George Spratt of Washington County, thanking him for services rendered during that happy vacation respite. Jefferson Davis was nothing if not the gracious southern gentleman.

And Maine? Well, we still have wonderful summers that continue to attract tourists from all over.

# 7

# Two Right Arms

## *Hell as Depicted by Old-Fashioned Standards*

In April 2004, the Damariscotta Historical Society published a column in the *Lincoln County News* containing a reprint of an old newspaper article found in one of its scrapbooks. It called the article "Two Right Arms" and could not or did not cite a date or newspaper of origin. Most probably the original newspaper in question was also the same *Lincoln County News*, published for over 130 years in Waldoboro and, now, Damariscotta, Maine. The paper was a veritable gold mine of stories and letters from Civil War veterans at the end of the nineteenth century, largely due to Samuel Miller, its owner and a veteran of the Twentieth Maine, Company E, who served as the historian of the Twentieth Maine Regimental Association.

The article in question recounts the story of two local citizens, both veterans who gave their right arms for their country while serving in different Maine volunteer regiments and, at the time of the original article, "living next door neighbors to each other" in the Round Top area of Damariscotta. Now the two old soldiers rest at opposite ends of a cemetery on Back Meadow Road, both minus their good right arms left behind on battlefields farther south.

## "The Extreme Left Man of the Entire Battle Line"

Abner Hiscock, sergeant in Company G, was a twenty-seven-year-old married mechanic when he enlisted in the Twentieth Maine in 1862. He lost his arm

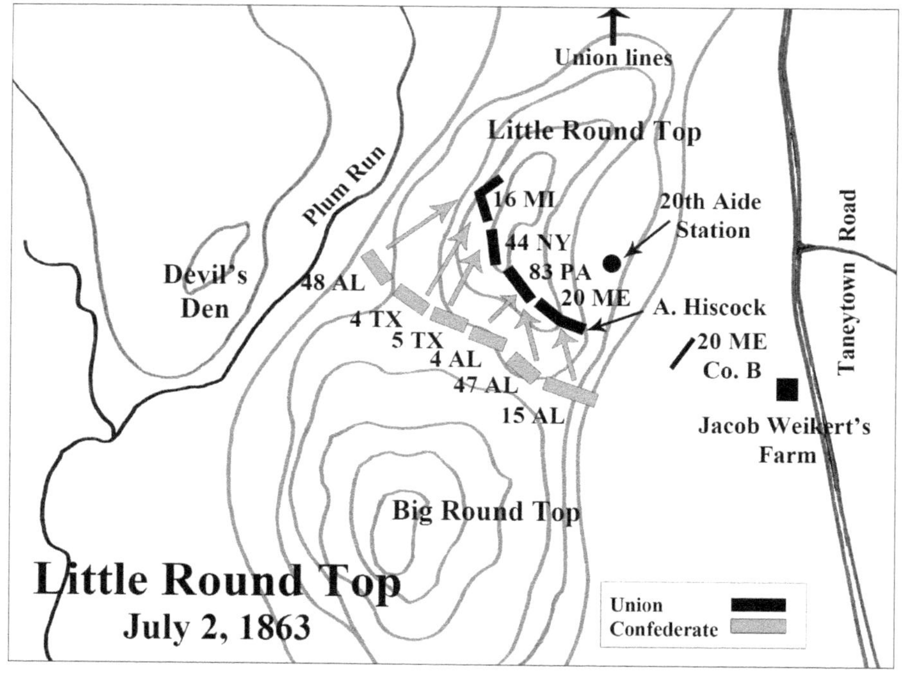


Author's map.

at Gettysburg. Hiscock, according to our newspaper article, was "the extreme left man of the entire battle line, left Guide of the left company of the left Regiment on Little Round Top, towards sundown of July 2nd, 1862 [*sic*]."

Although the story of the Twentieth has often been told and retold, sometimes less publicized and more personal accounts of a great event can add little bits to the story. Hiscock told the *News* reporter that Oates's Alabama regiment had just marched uphill to within twenty-five yards of his company lines. The account in the *News* is brief, but this would appear to be the Fifteenth Alabama's first assault on the Twentieth's far left just before that line was "refused," or bent back to cover the flank. Good descriptions of this battle abound, but perhaps the most comprehensive are John J. Pullen's classic *20th Maine* and Thomas Desjardin's *Stand Firm Ye Boys from Maine*.

Arriving only minutes ahead of the Alabamians, there was little time for the regiment to dig in. Chamberlain dispatched Company B down the slope to the southeast as an antiflanking measure and spread the other companies out in a line ending with G. The men of the Twentieth took what small cover could be had behind rocks and trees. As Oates's troops advanced uphill, the

Mainers rose up and fired a volley at the Alabamians that John Pullen wrote "lighted all the fires of hell in that hot, shadowed backyard of the battle." Hiscock fired his weapon with that volley as it momentarily stopped the Confederate advance and was almost immediately hit himself. He always felt that his attacker was aiming at the little white diamond on the sergeant's insignia on his sleeve (a common belief among wounded sergeants). This seems plausible in that the ball tore away his thumb knuckle where his right hand held his rifle up by his face and then traveled on just a bit farther to shatter his bent arm just above the elbow. Certainly this was a close brush with sudden death; the Minié ball mangled the arm that was within inches of his head.

That was it; Abner Hiscock's battle was over, his war was over, but he did not fall on the field. Remaining on his feet, he lit out for the Twentieth's aid station. Who knows what was going through Hiscock's mind, whether he thought he would die or whether he would live—with or without his arm. He must have realized that the sooner he sought medical attention the better his chance of survival.

Timothy O'Sullivan's "Breastworks on Little Round Top; Round Top in Distance" (July 1863) appears to show the Twentieth's position in the middle distance. *Library of Congress.*

The Twentieth Maine's aid station was established by John Chamberlain and a few orderlies in an out-of-the-way area on the backside of Little Round Top. This youngest Chamberlain had recently graduated from Bowdoin and visiting his brothers Joshua and Tom. Probably John's brother, the colonel, was looking for a safe place for John during the coming battle. With no medical training or life experience to help him, John Chamberlain did his best to help; the Twentieth had no surgeon on the field at Gettysburg. Hardly in a sheltered spot, the station was soon in danger of being shelled and was removed to Jacob Weikert's farm farther to the east on the Taneytown Road. It was some time before Hiscock caught up with them and found help. Abner Hiscock must have been a cussed-tough man; he may have left the field of battle with his right arm mangled, but he left on his own two feet. He carried his rifle with him all the way to the rear with his good left arm.

## "SOMETHING BIG WAS GOING ON, AND A MAN FELT HE OUGHT TO BE PART OF IT"

Hiscock's neighbor Thomas Arnold served two enlistments: first as a private in the Twenty-first Maine from October 1862 to August 1863 and second as a corporal in the Thirty-second Maine in 1864 and 1865. Arnold is listed as a farmer, born in Bremen in 1848, nineteen years old at the time of his enlistment in the Twenty-first and twenty when he reenlisted in the Thirty-second. (The math gets even funkier with the addition of a birth date of 1845 on his gravestone and ages of thirty-two in the 1880 census and sixty-six in the 1910 census.) The Thirty-second was known to have scraped the bottom of the barrel with perhaps more members under the minimum age of eighteen than any other regiment. Maybe Arnold didn't know his birth date, not uncommon at the time, but more likely he lied at least once to get into the service, didn't keep track of what he said and so contradicted himself in later years.

Despite combat service at Port Hudson, Louisiana, with the Twenty-first (a nine-month regiment that was one of the first Union regiments to pass up the Mississippi through the Delta as part of the Banks expedition), Thomas Arnold was either patriotic enough or adventurous enough to enlist twice. More than likely, there were strong economic motivators as well. By 1864, "volunteer" was somewhat of a misnomer; state enlistment quotas, the draft and bounties played a large part in filling the ranks.

Reenlisting veterans like Arnold could reap at least $700 in federal and state bounties; rich men avoiding the draft by paying for a substitute could further sweeten the pot. Arnold might have believed he could finance his future and that he had a good chance of survival. He didn't realize the price would be his good right arm.

Because the story of the Thirty-second is less well known, we'll spend a little time describing its history and the battle in which Tom Arnold lost his arm. The Thirty-second does not rate a place of its own on William F. Fox's esteemed list of Three Hundred Fighting Regiments, as did eleven other Maine regiments, including the Twentieth, the First Maine Cavalry and the First Maine Heavy Artillery. However, the Thirty-second is notable as Maine's last Civil War regiment and one that virtually fought itself out of existence. The enlisted men might have been mere boys, but the officers were generally capable and at least somewhat experienced. Colonel Mark F. Wentworth and a number of his junior officers had previously served in the Twenty-seventh Maine, a nine-month regiment that saw virtually no action beyond picket duty in Virginia and around Washington. The Twenty-seventh's claim to fame was that 315 men stayed behind to guard Washington, D.C., during the Gettysburg crisis while the rest of the regiment mustered out and headed for home. A grateful War Department awarded the men of the Twenty-seventh the Congressional Medal of Honor for standing ready to protect the all but deserted capital in case of a Union defeat at Gettysburg. Medal or not, Wentworth, according to John Pullen in *Shower of Stars*, felt cheated out of living "one of the great experiences of his generation." He and many other officers from the Twenty-seventh petitioned Augusta for assignment in a new regiment. The Thirty-second was both their first available and their last opportunity.

Wentworth began assembling his regiment at Camp Keyes in Augusta during the winter of 1864. Training was hampered by deep snows. Before the troops were sufficiently drilled and even before all the companies were organized, the Thirty-second was shipped south to join Grant's army. On May 5, when Thomas Arnold was mustered into Company I, a Newcastle regiment captained by Marcus L. Hussey, Companies A through F and their sister regiment, the Thirty-first Maine, had already joined the Second Brigade, Second Division, Ninth Corps, commanded by Ambrose E. Burnside. Arnold missed the battles at the Wilderness and Spotsylvania Courthouse but caught up with his regiment on May 25 when the last companies, G through I, joined the Thirty-second. Less than three weeks later, after horrifying fighting at Cold Harbor and after little more than a month in the field, the regiment was no longer untrained and untried. The boys of the Thirty-second were veterans now. According to Pullen, the regiment was down to "only about three hundred and fifty muskets" according to Wentworth with "125 killed and wounded" according to Adjunct Calvin Hayes. This was just the beginning.

After Cold Harbor, Grant moved his armies up to the outskirts of Petersburg in a fast-paced and grueling march of thirty-five miles, but he failed to make quick work of grabbing up Petersburg. Instead, his army, including the Thirty-second, went all but underground, building a maze of trenches and bomb proofs facing their foes, who were also hunkered down in a similar string of fortresses and trenches. It was a whole new kind of warfare for the two armies.

## "JOHNNY, YOU'RE GOING TO HEAVEN!"

Early in July, Burnside and a group of coal miners from the Forty-eighth Pennsylvania hatched a plot to dig a five-hundred-foot tunnel under a Confederate fort called Elliot's Salient on the line to their front, fill it with four hundred tons of gunpowder and blow a hole big enough for the army to charge through and take Cemetery Ridge with its command of Petersburg. It was, according to historian Bruce Catton, "an unorthodox idea brought forward by amateurs." Since the debacle at Fredericksburg in 1862, General Ambrose Burnside was a man with little credibility. Grant's high command was not enthusiastic; their immediate plans were centered more on Hancock and the Second Corps crossing the James at Deep Bottom and Sheridan's cavalry using this movement as a screen to cover an end run to cut the Virginia Central Railroad and Lee's communications close to Richmond. The Confederate capital was, after all, the real objective; as the capital's supply center, Petersburg was just a backdoor opportunity. As Lee blocked Grant's efforts, the tunnel was suddenly far more acceptable to the Union command because Lee had left behind only three divisions to hold five miles of Petersburg trenches. The other five-eighths of his army had been diverted to stop Hancock and Sheridan. The gunpowder plot appeared to be a golden opportunity that hindsight tells us might have ended the war months earlier. The time was ripe to make a decisive attack on Lee, and the tunnel, originally thought to be only a diversion to keep the soldiers busy, would provide the access.

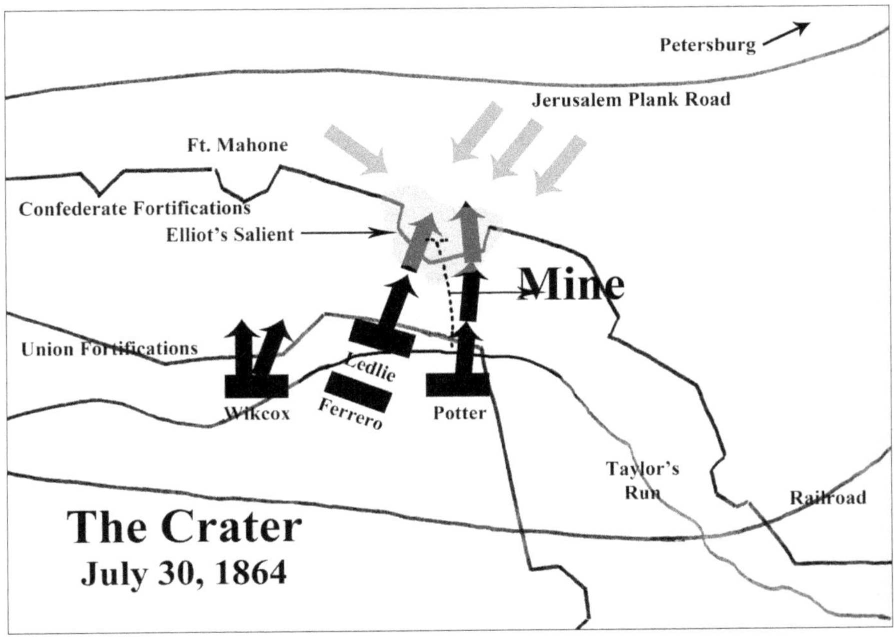


Author's map.

The five-hundred-foot-long tunnel, dug by hand, was not a quick and easy project. There was ample opportunity for the tunnel plans to be discovered. The Federal command thought from the start that the Confederates might discover the plot and tunnel in from their side to thwart the plan. To be sure, something was known but nothing definite that could be acted upon. Pullen claims that Union pickets would catcall their Confederate counterparts, yelling, "Johnny, you're going to heaven!" News of a gunpowder plot even reached home. According to Henry Houston's regimental history, Sergeant Hilling of Company G wrote home to the newspapers in Bath regularly with news of the Thirty-second. He began his postexplosion letter with this line: "In a former letter, I informed you that something was going on that would one day make the rebels tremble," indicating he had spilled the beans at least cryptically sometime before. Rumors were ripe even in the Confederate capital. On the very morning of the explosion, according to Pullen, the *Portsmouth (NH) Journal* reprinted a story from the *Richmond (VA) Whig* that spread the impending plan across seacoast New Hampshire and southern Maine. The *Whig*'s writer predicted the destruction of Petersburg from a blast from the "infernal regions" and further prophesized, "I tremble to think of it. Perhaps a few hours will bring the dreadful realization." By the time very many people in Colonel Wentworth's hometown of Kittery read the *Journal* article, the damage was already done.

Grant assigned George Meade the duty of finalizing the plans. After the blast, Burnside's four divisions were to move in four waves across the field. The first would secure the trenches on each side of the targeted fort to protect the projected opening in the lines from flanking, and then the successive waves would make the push to Cemetery Ridge. And of course, speed was necessary. The plan was not the problem, but execution of the plan was a disaster.

For such a promising idea, the opportunity for error was fully exploited by all involved. Animosity between Meade and Burnside led to confusion and poor communications. Because they were fresh, Burnside planned for Edward Ferrero's Negro troops to lead the way, but Meade was conflicted and changed the battle order at the last moment. He did not trust the black troops, but he also wanted to avoid the racial criticism of sacrificing them if things went wrong with the attack. Meade told Burnside to pick another division to lead out. Straws were literally drawn, and the First Division commanded by General James Ledlie, a drunk and incompetent, won the draw. On the morning of the explosion, Ledlie went into a dugout behind the lines to drink without first giving any orders to his troops. Ledlie was not alone in his absence; Ferrero was with him. Furthermore, very few officers of rank were on the field that day. Then, Meade ordered Burnside to remove impediments to the advance of the troops through the Federal lines. In particular he wanted the eight-foot-deep log-and-dirt trench leveled and the barrier of abattis (felled trees and sharpened sticks) in front of it removed in the dark of the night before the attack. This would allow the battle lines to form up and the divisions to sweep across the field in formation and through the newly exploded gap in the Rebel lines. Incredibly, impossibly, Burnside did not follow through with this major preparation, and nobody from the high command checked. The mistakes of Burnside and his command would soon destroy the Thirty-second and much of the Ninth Corps.

## "The Wholly Unexpected Site So Much Resembling the Day of Judgment"

The divisions were moved into position in the staging area during the night; Houston says the Thirty-second was placed directly in front of the targeted fort. The explosion was planned for around 3:30 a.m., but the fuse went out somewhere along the five hundred feet. Not knowing if the powder would ignite at any second, two poor suckers had to go in and relight the fuse. Just before five o'clock on the morning of June 30, 1864, the relit fuse finally touched off, and the explosion that followed was incredible. Sergeant Hilling of the Thirty-second described the results: "With one deafening roar that caused the earth to shake, the fort was blown to a confused mass of ruin." Other observers described the event with a little more excitement as a rumbling sound followed by a shaking of the earth like an earthquake. "Tremendous" is the operative word for the explosion that followed. According to Pullen, one observer wrote, "With a tremendous explosion, a conical mountain, seemingly half an acre in extent, rose in the air." Another said, according to Catton, that it was "a tremendous blast which rent the sleeping hills beyond, a vast column of earth and smoke shoots upward to a great height, its dark sides flashing out sparks of fire, hangs poised for a moment in mid-air, and then hurtling downward with a roaring sound, showers of stones, broken timbers and blackened human limbs." It must have been frightening, deafening and stunningly concussive.

*Before Petersburg at Sunrise, July 30th 1864* by Alfred Waud. The explosion is at the top, just right of the center, with the mine entrance below it at midpage but farther to the right. *Library of Congress.*

Pullen described the scene: the blast left a crater 170 feet long, 80 feet wide and 30 feet deep. The sides sloped down to a jagged and littered bottom. There was no sign, beyond a few pieces, of the two-hundred-odd Confederates who were moments before sleeping in the fort. Furthermore, troops in trenches for up to a quarter mile on either side of the former fort fled "in terror from the wholly unexpected site so much resembling the Day of Judgment." The dust settled somewhat, and within minutes of the mine explosion, the Federal batteries opened up on any Confederate position left that could fire on the advancing troops. The field was perfectly prepared for Burnside with a huge, new, empty space between his troops and Cemetery Ridge.

Then things began to go wrong: the divisions could not advance through their own lines. The attackers were hemmed in by their own trenches. No battle lines were formed when the men of Ledlie's First Division finally straggled by twos and threes through a ten-foot-wide opening in the defenses and hightailed it directly into the crater that they recognized as (and Bruce Catton named it) "the great-grandfather of all rifle pits." They knew a safe harbor when they saw one and poured into the crater by the hundreds. The men did not know Meade's grand plan or what part they were supposed to play; they'd had no particular orders. Nobody was shooting at them yet, but these men knew the failings of their leadership, and surely a nice, deep, ready-made hole would come in handy. The crater was soon filled with troops. There was not a single division commander on the field and hardly anyone else of sufficient rank to take charge or to move the men out to strategic locations. Later, both Grant and Confederate general William Mahone acknowledged that this lack of leadership was a critical failing.

On the whole, the operation was so slow off the mark and so disorganized that Mahone's Confederates had time to recover from their shock, regroup, reinforce and open fire on their attackers. A whole hour, according to Catton, had quickly passed since the explosion. An attack that should have taken fifteen minutes and been virtually unopposed was bogged down in a hole in the ground. The Confederates used their time well. "Our batteries and those of the enemy were now in full play, and with rifle firing the din was deafening," wrote Sergeant Hilling. "Shot and shell flew thick and fast. It was truly terrific. Two or three forts were firing upon us, while our forts were firing on them and the town of Petersburg, part of which was set on fire." It was the largest artillery barrage of the war. The growing number of Federal troops were soon pinned down in their big rifle pit by a crossfire from the trenches, which they had neglected to occupy, on either side of the crater.

## "A Trip to Hell as It Was Depicted by Old Fashioned Standards"

The Thirty-second's brigade was to move to the right of the crater. Wentworth somehow managed to get his regiment disentangled from their own trenches, Hiller recorded, "and with cheer upon cheer, amidst a shower of shot and grape, we rushed into the ruins. It was some time before we could see many feet in advance, the smoke of powder being almost blinding as well as nearly suffocating." From what little could be seen, there was no cause to cheer. Pullen describes the scene most vividly as "infernally scary" in which "live and dead Confederate soldiers lay in various stages of burial in and around the crater—some with feet, others with heads or arms sticking out of the churned up earth. There were also pieces of people scattered about, unthinkable slippery things underfoot." Furthermore, the ground had not settled completely; Pullen wrote that it "kept rising in spurts as though raked by the claws of a giant invisible cat." It is little wonder that almost every account of the Battle of the Crater is chock-full of allusions to hell and the demonic. Arnold himself told the *News* reporter that the whole charge was "a trip to hell as it was depicted by old fashioned standards."

*Scene of the Explosion* by Alfred Waud showing the advance to the "crater" after the explosion with the mounds it caused in the middle distance. *Library of Congress.*

With Colonel Wentworth in the lead, the Thirty-second scrambled as a loose mass, not a line, into the area of the crater and perhaps through the crater itself. Both Hilling and Arnold refer to "the fort," "the crater" and the line of "defenses" almost interchangeably in their descriptions. It is unlikely that anyone who was there actually knew where they were—the smoke and dust were very thick, and even if they could see, the landscape around them had radically changed with the explosion. Somewhere in this confusion, a Union general appeared out of the smoke and dirt to compliment Wentworth for leading his own men into battle; they were two of the few officers on the scene. In the pursuit of glory, honor or some penultimate experience, Wentworth didn't have time for this. With only a moment of confusion in the bizarre landscape, Wentworth, trailing his men behind him, pushed out again. According to Hiller:

> *We were soon with Col. Wentworth through the fort, over the backs or bodies of some other regiments, who were in the fort and lying down. We passed on, over massive blocks of earth, dead bodies of rebels and the debris which the explosion caused, and into the farthest line of the rebel works, where we planted our flag or what remained of it.*

Arnold claimed it was a charge of "half a mile through mini [*sic*] balls" in which "death reaped his awful harvest all about." Somewhere along the way, Arnold's friend Henry Page fell dead at his feet.

At this point, as the Thirty-second went over the second line of Rebel defenses about two hundred yards behind the crater, things rapidly fell apart. For a minute or so, they held about two hundred yards or so of Rebel trenches. If other regiments had followed them beyond the crater perhaps the battle could have been redeemed, but this was not to be the case. They were out in front, basically alone and soon confronted with a counterattack. Hilling said, "Before it was fairly planted, the staff was shot in two, and the flag, what was remaining of it, was literally cut to pieces." (The remains of the flag are really quite amazing, although many pieces were cut away by the troops themselves to prevent the flag from being captured. It can be seen at the Maine State Museum in Augusta.) Then, Wentworth was shot twice; one ball went through his left side with such force that it blew off a piece of hip bone and then went on to mangle the arm of Company G's eighteen-year-old sergeant Ray P. Eaton, who was behind him. As Hilling describes it, their downed leader still cheered his men on. The man remembers entirely too much cheering for the center of hell.

Tom Arnold was also hit just as he went over this second line of defenses. He told the *News* that it felt like "the sting of a bee." He was probably hit by flanking fire from the counterattack. The ball either went through his arm and across his chest or vice versa. He claimed that, at the time, the furrow the bullet made across his chest hurt more than his arm. Like Hiscock, he knew his fighting was done, but Tom Arnold dropped his gun, grabbed his shattered right arm in his good left hand and lit out "like a fox" for the rear. At the first line of defenses (probably the crater itself), he said that "he went over the breast works head first and was put on his feet, by an officer who cut away his belts and relieved him of his load of ammunition. Sixty rounds in his belt and two packages in his pocket."

His comrades in the Thirty-second soon withdrew back to the crater themselves, carrying their wounded colonel with them. Wentworth, according to Pullen, was deposited next to Lieutenant James Chase of the Thirty-second, a sight he remembered for the rest of his life. Chase had been hit behind the left eye with a force that nearly blew the eyeball out of the socket and left it dangling in a bloody mess. The wound did not look promising, and Wentworth, himself a physician, felt there was little chance of the young man's survival. Wentworth, Chase and Tom Arnold, along with many other members of the Thirty-second, needed immediate medical attention. The Rebels were quickly solidifying their control over the field of battle, and safe passage back to the Union lines looked nearly impossible.

There is no way of knowing what time it was when the Thirty-second reached the limit of their charge, but by 8:30 a.m., official accounts describe the area around the crater as a killing field. Grant called off the attack and all support to the men in the crater by 9:30 a.m., a decision that would not be known in that corner of hell until nearly 12:30 p.m. There were not many opportunities for escape, but it was decided to carry Wentworth back to the Federal trenches. Hilling recounts the dangerous return to Union lines with Wentworth and other wounded: "The shot flew round us thick and fast, but not a man of the detail was hurt. We got safely to the fort, placed our men in safety, and were about to return, when we heard that our men were repulsed and driven back over our front line of breastworks, and also that the 31$^{st}$ and 32$^{nd}$ Maine were all cut to pieces or prisoners."

Perhaps Arnold left the crater with such a stretcher detail; maybe he high-tailed it out by himself. He couldn't have remained behind for long or there would have been no escape. The remains of the Thirty-second endured several charges before the Confederates retook the area and the survivors were forced to surrender. This would be around 1:00 p.m. by official count.

The *News*'s reporter has Arnold remembering, "Rebs on all sides were yelling, 'Surrender, you damned Yanks,' and were shooting down men with revolvers at ten yards distance." Surely he wasn't in the crater at the end, but he would have had opportunity in later years to hear about it from survivors, perhaps from his own Company I's lieutenant George L. Hall of Nobleboro, who surrendered and spent six months as a prisoner of war.

## "A SORRY DAY'S WORK FOR US, AND NOTHING GAINED"

Houston, recording the casualties in the regimental history, quoted Adjutant Calvin Hayes, writing that evening after the disaster, "I have made my evening report; five officers wounded, eight missing, and eight men killed, thirty-one wounded, and seventy-six missing. A sorry day's work for us, and nothing gained." He was now in charge of the Thirty-second. On Sunday the thirty-first, after the numbers firmed up, he wrote again, "Everything looks so lonesome. So many have gone; one hundred and twenty-eight killed, wounded, and missing out of less than one hundred and fifty who went into the fight. Out of sixteen officers who were engaged, three escaped unharmed. We have now in the regiment eighty-five men, including cooks, present sick, and extra duty men." Hilling gives a similar count in his letter to Bath detailing Company G casualties and describing wounds consistently as "not dangerous" or "we fear mortally wounded" or "since died." He knew that people at home needed to know names and tried to give as many as possible.

The fiasco at the crater was investigated by a Court of Inquiry, and it was found about four thousand men died due to the gross incompetence of its leadership. Deservedly, Burnside and Ledlie took the brunt of the blame. Burnside was relieved of command and went on (permanent) leave. Ledlie was released from the service. Grant and Meade also took some heat from the Committee on the Conduct of the War. Owning responsibility, Grant testified before the committee, "I think the cause of the disaster was simply leaving the passage of orders from one to another down to an inefficient man. I blame his seniors also for not seeing that he did his duty, all the way up to myself."

In December, the Thirty-second, practically nonexistent as a fighting force on its own, was combined with the Thirty-first Maine. Arnold's captain Marcus Hussey was mustered out at the time of the consolidation.

Personally, he had probably had enough; he had lost two children at home to childhood disease during the previous July. The second died on the very day of the Battle of the Crater. He had a lot to go home to; in October, his wife delivered a new baby boy. Despite his wishes to return to service, Colonel Mark F. Wentworth resigned in October due to his wounds but was promoted to brevet brigadier general in March 1865. Amazingly, the young Lieutenant Chase, last seen with the bloody face and mangled eye, recovered and returned (with a glass eye) to fight another day.

## "THE DREADFUL MINNIE BALL"

Both Hiscock and Arnold were undone by "the dreadful minnie ball," which the Civil War Society calls the most common small arms ammunition. The two men were not alone; this heavy, soft lead bullet was the number one cause of all wounds, followed by various artillery projectiles and shrapnel, sabers and bayonets. Jenny Goellnitz in her treatise on Civil War Medicine described the disastrous effects. The Minié ball could kill on the field at one thousand feet but was even more likely to cause death at a later date just from the effects of the extreme damage it inflicted. When it hit bone, the lead expanded, shattering and splintering the bone. When it hit soft tissue, it mangled and tore up muscle and skin, blood vessels and organs. Head and body shots were most likely fatal; shots to the extremities could frequently be remedied, despite the extent of damaged bone and muscle, by amputation. Fortunately for many soldiers, at least 70 percent of all wounds were to the extremities. Unfortunately, these resulted in some thirty thousand amputations to Federal soldiers alone.

Tom Arnold thought the crater was hell, but what came next for both Hiscock and himself was surely the devil's workshop. In the general run of things, regimental surgeons set up shop under tents or in nearby barns, churches and other buildings. During and immediately after battles, there were often so many wounded that there was not enough room under cover for all. The wounded would often end up spread out on the ground around the surgeons' work areas. If they were lucky, there might be trees or some other protection from the sun and the elements. The numbers of wounded alone necessitated the need to sort out the wounded by likelihood of survival. Wounds to the body or head would wait in favor of amputations that were performed quickly and often without much speculation over saving the arm or leg in question.

Minié ball with scale. From the author's collection. *David Higgins photo.*

Jacob Weikert's Farm at Gettysburg provides a good example of how field hospitals worked. The Union army had a fairly organized system for moving men off the battlefield, through the aid stations and into the field hospitals involving stretcher details and ambulances. Walking wounded, like Hiscock, were probably afraid to stop and depended on their own two feet despite the distance. Dr. John Billings of the Second Division, Fifth Corps, established the field hospital at Weikert's Farm on the Taneytown Road while the Twentieth's own Company B, hidden behind a stone wall, was engaging flankers within sight just across the field. Soon, Desjardin says, the huge barn was filled with wounded lying on straw, and outside there were long lines of wounded men on the ground with no shelter. By the time the day's nasty work was completed, Billings and his staff had treated more than seven hundred, most suffering from bullet wounds.

After moving men down from the aid station on the backside of Little Round Top, Desjardin writes, John Chamberlain remained to help with the wounded. He was truly shocked by the field hospital's conditions. He wrote, "Men without an eye or nose or leg or arm or with a mangled head or body would constantly attract your sympathy, each one looking worse than the one that went before." It was soon evident that the most important thing he could do to help was to rig makeshift shelters of blankets and sticks to shade the wounded from the unmerciful sun. The men of the Twentieth had no regimental surgeon at Gettysburg and had to suffer and wait until another surgeon could see to them. Making the rounds, John Chamberlain came across Lieutenant Kendall of the Twentieth lying untreated with a bullet wound to the neck. Chamberlain convinced an assistant to remove the bullet, but the officer soon died anyway. Kendall had certainly been skipped over by the surgeons as likely to die.

## "In the Horrid Heap He Recognized His Own Good Right Arm"

Civil War surgeons are often castigated as butchers and sawbones; the latter name is actually derived from the surgeon's amputation saw. On the whole, most were untrained or barely trained in surgery and certainly unprepared to perform thousands of operations under the worst conditions. Given the pace, quantity and conditions of the surgery, most Civil War surgeons did the best they could under disheartening conditions and surely do not deserve derision.

Goellnitz says that, contrary to common understanding, soldiers were not generally conscious during surgery. Chloroform was quite readily available and used to render the wounded unconscious. On the other hand, antiseptic procedures were definitely not practiced. Joseph Lister's discoveries and work in bacteriology were not known until after the war ended. Some small attempts at cleanliness were made; instruments were rinsed, sponges and cloths wrung out in (often bloody) water and hands washed on occasion, but nothing was sterile or hardly even clean. The doctors did not know any better; the caseload was huge and often the conditions were too frantic for anyone to give a thought to cleaning up. And so germs became the invisible enemy, and infection was the rampant killer of thousands of wounded men who might have survived if doctors had known more.

Carl Shurz, in his *Reminiscences* reprinted on the Civil War Medicine site, provides a bloodthirsty vision of surgery at Gettysburg:

> *There stood the surgeons, their sleeves rolled up to the elbows, their bare arms as well as their linen aprons smeared with blood, their knives not*

An amputation being performed at Gettysburg. The surgeon is in the center with a knife while the patient is being held down on the table behind him. *National Archives and Records Administration.*

> *seldom held between their teeth, while they were helping a patient on or off the table, or had their hands otherwise occupied; around them pools of blood and amputated arms or legs in heaps, sometimes more than* [a] *man-high. Antiseptic methods were still unknown at that time. As a wounded man was lifted on the table, often shrieking with pain as the attendants handled him, the surgeon quickly examined the wound and resolved upon cutting off the injured limb. Some ether was administered and the body put in position in a moment. The surgeon snatched his knife from between his teeth, where it had been while his hands were busy, wiped it rapidly once or twice across his blood-stained apron, and the cutting began. The operation accomplished, the surgeon would look around with a deep sigh, and then—"Next!"*

The general amputation procedure (as described by Goellnitz) was to remove the bullet (if present) and to clean the wound of dirt, cloth, bone fragments and foreign matter with a sponge, rag or even the surgeon's fingers. Then the surgeon would use a scalpel to cut away the skin above and below the wound, leaving a flap of skin to stretch over the stump. Next he would saw through the bone with a bone saw and slice away any remaining muscle. With the appendage removed, he would tie off any major blood vessels with (unsterilized) thread, silk or horsehair and sew the flap in place, leaving a hole for drainage of the wound. The threads would be left with long ends dangling so they could be pulled loose when the vessels had healed shut. The stump would be bandaged and sometimes covered in a plaster cast. The whole operation might take ten minutes. Recovery would be left in the hands of God.

Hiscock was lucky; his life must have seemed salvageable, and within only an hour or so, his good right arm was amputated. He was not alone. Desjardin writes that Dr. Billings and the surgeons from two regiments "undertook the task of sawing parts off soldiers bodies until piles of amputated limbs reached higher than the fence outside the house." Under the hot July sun, the smell alone became unbearable. Hiscock could attest to the size of this pile (and probably the smell also): he told the *News* reporter, "On recovering from the ether the first sight that met his eyes was a pile of arms and legs as large as a small hay cock. In the horrid heap he recognized his own good right arm, by the shattered knuckle where the mini [*sic*] ball first hit him."

## "I NEVER DID DIE YET!"

Generally speaking, a wounded soldier would not often wait more than twenty-four to forty-eight hours to be seen by a surgeon. Perhaps because the Battle of the Crater produced so many wounded, Tom Arnold's arm was not attended to for fourteen days. Three days after he was shot, he was transported with other wounded to City Point. An incredible eleven days after that, his arm was finally amputated. This was simply neglect; the wound was crawling with maggots that Arnold said caused an "unbearable itching." As maggots eat only dead flesh, this may have been a good thing. Even so, his arm was in such a state that the operating surgeon, a man named Sheldon, said, "He can't live." Arnold, despite his deteriorating condition, spoke right up, "I never did die yet." After the operation, a Dr. True saw Arnold sitting up and smoking a pipe and said with admiration, "He's a Maine man; you can't kill him. You might take a leg and he'd still survive."

After a battle and as soon as they could be stabilized, wounded men were moved out of field hospitals, often by train or steamboat, to general hospitals behind the lines and as far away as major cities like Washington, Philadelphia and New York. Those strong enough to move were taken away first. The seriously wounded were often left behind to die in battlefield hospitals days or even weeks later. Tom Arnold, it would appear, was taken to Washington. Hiscock may have been moved to Satterlee Hospital in Philadelphia, as there is some record of men of the Twentieth treated there after Gettysburg. Eventually, wounded soldiers would be patched up enough to return to their regiments, or they were shipped out to their home states. In Maine, many wounded men in need of further care were sent to Cony Hospital in Augusta in what could be considered a precursor to the Togus Veterans Hospital.

## "A VAST, HIDDEN ARMY WHICH WAS THE GREATEST ENEMY OF BOTH SIDES IN THE CIVIL WAR"

Although many surgeons thought there was a relationship between cleanliness and infection rates, they did not have the knowledge or means to create sterile conditions. As a consequence, germs were passed from one patient to the next by the very people who were trying to help them. Pullen describes bacteria as "a vast, hidden army which was the greatest enemy of both sides in the Civil War." The infections that developed in wounded men after surgery were termed "surgical fevers" and manifested themselves in several varieties.

Both Jenny Goellnitz and the Civil War Medicine site give graphic descriptions of the ravages of bacteria on amputees. One of the most deadly infections was pyemia, a form of blood poisoning whose name means "pus in the blood." Only about three out of one hundred men who developed pyemia survived. Today, we know the causes were "Staphylococcus aureus and Streptococcus pyogenes, bacterial cells which generate pus, destroy tissue, and release deadly toxins into the bloodstream." In the 1860s, treatment was hampered in part by the misconception that "laudible pus," or pus that was discharging freely from a wound, was a good thing. In the next stage of pyemia, the pus would suddenly dry up, and the victim would spike a fever. Instead of recognizing the progression of the infection, surgeons theorized that as long as the pus was present, things were good and thus laudable, which was hardly the case.

Other surgical fevers included tetanus, erysepilas (an acute infectious skin disease) and osteomyelitis (bone inflammation). And of course, there was the well-known and dreaded gangrene, a rotting away of the flesh that was no longer able to receive blood due to the obstructions or damage caused by wounds and surgery. Hospital gangrene, which is, thankfully, extinct today, began as a small black spot and soon spread throughout the wound, turning it into a rotten, smelly mess. With both surgical fevers and gangrene, multiple surgeries were often attempted to remove dead or dying flesh, improve leaking ligatures of blood vessels that were not healing properly and amputate infected bone. Each new surgery, performed on a man already in a debilitated state, increased the chances of infection and death.

Hiscock stayed in the hospital until January 19, 1864, growing worse all the time. Finally sent home on furlough, the poor man learned that his house had burned to the ground while he was gone, and the news had been kept from him. His family felt he had enough to worry about without this news. Seeking relief, Hiscock took his arm to Dr. Call of Newcastle. Hiscock told the *News* reporter that "the doctor looked at it, made some unconventional remarks and tore off the plaster and bandages which covered the stump. Relieved from the support, a cupful of puss gushed forth leaving a large cavity." Presumably, this would be diagnosed as "laudible pus" and place Hiscock dangerously in the developing stages of pyemia. Given the condition of the arm more than six months after the battle, Dr. Call advised a further operation. Hiscock was weak and did not feel he would survive another amputation. He was probably right; Goellnitz says that 52 percent of secondary amputations resulted in death. Under the good doctor's ministrations, Hiscock finally began to heal, but the stump remained tender for the rest of his life.

Arnold had other problems. The wound was not sufficiently probed for shattered bone, and he was plagued by "a splinter of bone which pricked him after the wound had healed." Dr. Bliss, who afterward attended President Garfield, offered to remove this for twenty-five dollars—big city prices. Instead Arnold, a frugal Yankee, went home on a fifteen-day leave and saw Damariscotta's own Dr. Dixon, who "removed the offending splinter which was about half an inch long. He charged one dollar for the job and there was never any trouble with it afterwards." Later in the article, Arnold admitted that "abscesses have made trouble for him to some extent ever since."

## "WHO WANTS TO SWAP A GOOD RIGHT ARM FOR $55 PER MONTH?"

Tom Arnold, despite the criminal treatment of his arm, was up and about within three months. He was finally discharged on March 3, 1865. Somewhere along the way, he became friendly with E.B. French, who was auditor of the Treasury in Washington, D.C. This landed him a job first as a messenger and later as a clerk for the Treasury Department, where he worked for twelve years before returning to Maine. Back home in Damariscotta, he supported himself as a mail carrier, a job in which one arm was sufficient. This supplemented the pension paid by a grateful government that was increased over the years from eight dollars a month to fifty-five dollars. But, wrote the *News* reporter, "Who wants to swap a good right arm for $55 per month?"

Tom Arnold did not come home alone. The *News* reporter must have had quite an enjoyable visit to the Arnold household and gives an account of marital bliss couched in terms of martial innuendo that is quite charming:

> *But Mr. Arnold says his experiences were not all to the bad for in Washington he besieged the heart of a Southern girl who was acting as a nurse for wounded Northern prisoners. In his attacks, he was more successful than at Petersburg. He finally brought Miss Gantt north with him as his wife. The lady had seven brothers in the Confederate Army, six of whom died for the Lost Cause. Mrs. Arnold says she wanted to make one Yankee suffer as much as they had made her suffer, but "Tommie" seems to enjoy his punishment and is as cheerful as a squirrel all the time.*

In the 1880 census, the same one that lists Tommie as thirty-two, Louisa E. Arnold was recorded as age twenty-seven and born in Virginia. This gives her a birth date of 1853 and makes her still a preteen at the end of the war, kind of young for a nurse. The Arnold gravestone lists her dates as 1845–1915, or nearly the same as her mathematically challenged husband. To further complicate things, the 1880 census shows a daughter, Cesstia, age ten, born in Washington, D.C., but the ever-contradictory stone records, "Their Neice Celestie Louisa Marsden 1872–." Despite their conviviality, the Arnolds remain a muddle that is unlikely to ever be resolved.

On the other hand, throughout the *Lincoln County News* article, the reader gets the idea that Abner Hiscock was a tough man and short on words. Only the bare bones of his story appear in the article, while Tom Arnold

"Tommie" Arnold's grave at Bethlehem Cemetery on Back Meadow Road in Damariscotta. *David Higgins photo.*

The Abner Hiscock family plot at Bethlehem Cemetery with Abner at the far right. *David Higgins photo.*

comes off as far more verbose. After his discharge, Hiscock went home to Damariscotta and presumably collected the same disability benefits as Arnold. Like Arnold, he supplemented his (probable) pension but not with a handicap-friendly job. Hiscock worked in the woods. As the *News* describes it, "This is pretty strenuous work for two good arms, but Mr. Hiscock with his left alone was the equal of any chopper in the business." A little more information can be gleaned from the Back Meadow Road Cemetery. If he had children, they might be buried among the numerous Hiscocks in this cemetery or in another graveyard elsewhere. Hiscock's own plot holds just four people: Abner and his three wives. He was either lucky in love or a ladies' man—tall, dark and silent?

# 8

# *William* and *Hattie*

## *Maine Sailing Ships in the Great War*

The turn of the twentieth century is such an interesting period. On one hand, science, invention and technology were advancing at a rapid rate, but on the other, the knowledge and application of these advances spread much more slowly than they do today. Throw in a war, and you have some pretty strange things going on. During World War I, the first bomber aircrafts dropped rocks over the side on the enemy below in an interesting combination of high-tech delivery of a Stone Age weapon. The myth of Polish cavalry charges on Bolshevik and, later, Nazi tanks has been debunked even though they maintained and successfully used these cavalry units up into World War II. Armored cars, tanks, submachine guns, automatic rifles, poison gas and the first serious use of submarines in warfare quickly developed. German U-boats bring us to our story of odd confrontations between Maine sailing ships and the German navy.

## "A Great and Prosperous Merchant Marine Is Indispensable"

Few people now realize that the United States merchant marine experienced a long decline between the end of the Civil War and World War I. There were a number of reasons for this, including the high cost of marine insurance, a lack of professionally trained merchant marines, legal and economic

Maine senator William P. Frye (1830–1911) served more than thirty years in Washington. *Library of Congress.*

procedures and a failure to embrace the new shipping technologies of steel and steam. Despite the efforts of Maine representative John Lynch and senator William P. Frye, Congress was unable to provide much in the way of remedies to the situation.

Although Great Britain was again dominating the seas with steel merchant ships driven by steam, Maine forestalled some of the national economic disaster by building the Downeasters, tough, fast, wooden sailing ships built to carry huge cargos great distances without the need to refuel. For a time, they did very well, especially in the Pacific trade where distances where huge and there were few places to take on coal. In addition, the coastal and intercoastal shipping markets also continued to do well enough despite incursions by the railroads. These were more or less niche markets in a changing industry.

The real problem lay with the Atlantic shipping industry, both imports and exports. As Theodore Roosevelt told Congress in 1905, "To the spread of our trade in peace and the defense of our flag in war a great and prosperous merchant marine is indispensable. We should have ships of our own and seamen of our own to convey our goods to neutral markets, and in case of need to reinforce our battle line." This seems logical now, but despite the efforts of Roosevelt and others, no one was able to put together legislation or procedures that would build the necessary merchant marine. In their book *In Peace and War*, Cruikshank and Kline say that by the beginning of the war in Europe in 1914, nearly 90 percent of U.S. shipping was conducted by foreign ships. The transportation of goods became a real issue for the United States as European navies pulled their merchant fleets and seamen home for war duties.

By this time, it was nearly too late for Maine's wooden shipbuilding industry, and it would take some effort to retool for steel and iron ships. The Thomaston yards, for example, were virtually closed between 1905 and 1917, overgrown with brush and empty. Town historian Aubigne Packard says that with a little cleanup and some training by older shipwrights, they were able to produce "9 schooners, one steamer, two barkentines" between 1917 and 1920. Money was to be made in shipping again. Bath built twenty-seven ships. In this period, other towns up and down the coast added more than sixty for a grand total of around one hundred largely wooden three- or four-masted schooners. Wood was what we did best. This was hardly a return to the halcyon days of Maine shipbuilding, but it was a respectable output.

William Baker's *Maritime History of Bath* describes that city's experience as different in that General Thomas Hyde began his business in foundries and marine engines in the second half of the nineteenth century. From there, he won a bid for the production of two steel gunboats powered by his triple-expansion engines in 1890, and Bath Iron Works began its long history of iron and steel shipbuilding. Taking a different tack, Arthur Sewell

The *William P. Frye* built by the Arthur Sewell & Company of Bath, Maine, in 1901. *Library of Congress.*

& Company, also of Bath, used a design by British naval architect J.F. Waddington to build the *Dirigo,* a steel four-masted bark launched in 1894. Although the acquisition of steel and the design itself proved problematic, Eugene Chamberlain, the U.S. commissioner of navigation, wrote, "The construction of this vessel marks the beginning of a new industry in this country. The ship of the future is to be of steel, and the introduction of that material is necessary to the maintenance for foreign trade of a fleet of large sailing vessels." The *Dirigo* did good duty as a merchant ship until 1917, when it was sunk in the English Channel by a German U-boat.

The Sewell Company went forward with this "new industry" and, refining the design, built nine more steel sailing ships. Although these ships did solid work transporting goods, they were not held in particularly high esteem by mariners. The Sewell Company kept changing the proportions of the hulls generally by making them longer but not wider. The essentially English-style hull was topped by Downeaster masts, sails and rigging. All features together were not the best combination for handling and speed.

## "Evidently the Grain Was Not Being Thrown Overboard Fast Enough"

The last of the Sewell steel four-masters was the *William P. Frye*, built and subsequently operated for the company's own account at a cost of around $150,000. Launched on October 3, 1901, the *Frye* was named after longtime Maine senator William Frye, that diligent supporter of American shipping. As described by Basil Lubbock in his book *The Downeasters*, the *Frye* measured out at 3,374 tons and 332 feet, 4 inches in length; it was not a high-performance ship but managed to ply its trade largely between the East Coast and the Pacific for fourteen years.

Fairburn's *Merchant Sail* records the *Frye*'s last voyage, captained by H.H. Kiehne, as from Baltimore to Puget Sound Navy Yard with 5,051 tons of coal, arriving in 167 days on September 24, 1914. It then took up a load of 5,034 tons of wheat to be delivered at Queenstown (Cobh, Ireland), Falmouth or Plymouth, England. After an uneventful trip around the Horn and 82 days out, the *Frye* was at 29°45' S and 24°50 W' off the coast of Brazil when it was taken by the German commerce raider *Prinz Eitel Friedrich* on January 27, 1915. The *Frye* immediately became famous as America's first merchant ship sunk in the Great War even though the United States was neutral and not at war with anyone.

The SS *Prinz Eitel Friedrich* was a German passenger liner built in 1904 and spent its first ten years in service in the Far East. It was 153 meters long and 8,797 tons. When World War I began, the *Prinz Eitel* was converted into an auxiliary cruiser and equipped as a commerce raider. This meant that its job was to attack and disrupt merchant shipping, and it was quite successful at this for a short time. Between the start of the war in August 1914 and January 1915, it sank eleven ships for a total tonnage of 33,000.

As described in *The Merchant Navy* by Archibald Kurd, Captain Max Thierichens of the *Prinz Eitel* stopped the *Frye* and made inquiries as to the cargo and destination. The German felt that because the cargo was potentially headed to Plymouth, a fortified town, the grain therefore was contraband and could be seized. The American captain argued to no avail that America was a neutral country and the grain was not for military use. The *Frye* was soon boarded by German officers and men who began to pitch the grain overboard. Meanwhile, the *Prinz Eitel* took off in pursuit of another ship. Kiehne continues the story with the German ship's return:

> *Evidently the grain was not being thrown overboard fast enough to suit the German skipper, for he sent half a hundred men aboard soon afterwards, and the work went on for hours without interruption. However, it was slow at the best, and I was informed the next morning that my ship would be sent to the bottom. It was originally the intention of the German captain to leave enough cargo in the hold of the ship for ballast. That part of the grain was to be rendered useless by salt water.*

There was nothing Captain Kiehne could do or say. Kiehne, his wife and two sons and his crew were taken aboard the *Prinz Eitel*, where they were treated very cordially for the duration of the voyage. Mrs. Kiehne cried as the *Frye* was scuttled with explosives. Like many Maine women who sailed with their captain husbands, she must have felt that the *Frye* was her home.

Eight ships were sunk by the *Prinz Eitel* between January 27 and February 20, 1915, but the *Frye* was the only American ship. Then the Germans headed north and put in at Newport News. The *Prinz Eitel* was in deplorable shape and needed repairs, coal and provisions. It was carrying upward of three hundred captured crew members and passengers from the various captured ships. After all, the United States was a neutral country and would provide a safe harbor!

The German ship *Prinz Eitel Friedrich* as photographed between 1910 and 1915. *Library of Congress.*

Captain Kiehne reported in a newspaper article in the *Bangor Semiweekly News* that after the British ship *Willerby* was sunk on February 20, there was a marked change in attitude among the German officers. For nearly a month, the Germans chased down every puff of smoke on the horizon. Then Kiehne was asked about the best place to seek repairs; he gave them directions to Newport News. "From then on the *Friedrich* ran from everything," he said. "On the last three nights I knew that the officers were getting wireless from British cruisers. On the last two nights before passing into the Virginia capes the order to the crew was, 'Everybody to the guns; nobody to sleep.' On the last night two of the British cruisers were within ten miles of us." Yes, he felt quite confident that Captain Thierichens and his ship would never leave the U.S. harbor until the war was ended. The British were out there waiting for the *Prinz*.

Thierichens did indeed ask for internment of the ship, and the U.S. Navy took custody of it. The guns, radios and propulsion were disabled. There was some talk of repatriotizing the officers and crew. There was more talk about restitution from the German government for the cost of the ship and the cargo. It was a diplomatic issue, and the lawyers had at it. The United States wanted restitution of $228,059 for the ship, cargo and other damages and losses. On April 13, 1915, Germany agreed to make restitution to both ship and cargo owners but desired that the case be presented in prize court in order to establish the facts. The United States declined to have the case presented in a German prize court because the *Frye* was unquestionably a neutral ship carrying cargo not intended for military purposes and under international law Germany was obligated to pay. Back and forth they went. The American public was increasingly incensed over this attack on their neutrality. Then, on May 7, another blow was struck that pushed the *Frye* squabbling aside and ended any further negotiations for payment. The unarmed British passenger ship *Lusitania* was sunk. More than 1,000 people died, including 128 Americans. It was only a matter of time before America entered the war against Germany.

The *William P. Frye* was unfortunately the first American merchant ship sunk by Germans during the Great War. It was not the last. When America entered the war, its shores and coastline became vulnerable to attack by German submarines.

## "What Are You Trying to Do Captain? Are You Trying to Get Killed?"

Dunn & Elliot began as a sail loft on the Georges River waterfront of Thomaston. By 1880, the company expanded into shipping and shipbuilding. Dunn & Elliot built as many as thirty ships including, in 1920, the *Edna Hoyt*, the last five-masted schooner ever built. The *Edna Hoyt* was considered an attraction and drew crowds wherever it sailed. Another Dunn & Elliot ship was far more ordinary.

Aubigne Packard writes the story of the *Hattie Dunn* in her *Town That Went to Sea*. The *Hattie Dunn* was launched in 1884 at Thomaston. It was a three-master of 414 tons, and for the next thirty-four years, it made its way as an ordinary cargo ship. Its last captain and part owner was Charles E. Holbrook of Tenants Harbor, who likely expected there would be many years to come at the wheel of the *Hattie Dunn*. Then on May 23, 1918, it met its destiny in "an undersea rendezvous."

Holbrook and the *Dunn* were on their way from New York to Charleston, sailing "in ballast" or without a cargo and also without a radio. Reportedly, there were seven crew members aboard, all above the age of forty. The oldest was a seventy-two-year-old German cook who, ironically, left Europe to

The schooner *Hattie Dunn* as seen from U-boat 151 before the *Dunn* was sunk. *Packard.*

escape the war after twice being aboard ships that were torpedoed. Nobody aboard was particularly worried; the navy reported that no Germans were in the area.

As Packard described the demise of the *Dunn*, about thirty-five miles off the New Jersey coast, a submarine was spotted, but nobody was concerned. A shot was fired off the bow, but Holbrook thought it was an American sub at target practice. A second shot took his attention, and he finally turned and started to run. It was too late; the *Dunn* was overtaken by the sub. The German captain shouted to Holbrook, "What are you trying to do, Captain? Are you trying to get killed?" There was nothing for it but to surrender.

The *Hattie Dunn* was soon boarded by a boatload of Germans. The little crew was given ten minutes to save their personal effects. While they were doing so, the Germans placed bombs in the hold and over the side of the boat. The *Hattie Dunn* people were loaded into their own lifeboat with an armed guard and told to make their way to the sub. There was a tremendous explosion, and the *Hattie Dunn* went down, bow first. With that, the little schooner became famous; it was the first American vessel to be sunk in World War I by a German sub in American waters. It would not be the last.

## "THEY LOOKED LIKE BEARDED SCULPINS"

While the *Hattie Dunn* was being dealt with, the sub chased down another schooner, the brand-new *Hauppage* bound in ballast for Portland, Maine. It soon met the same fate as the *Dunn* and was left lying on its beams with a hole in its side. The *Dunn* crew was joined by the *Hauppage* crew aboard U-151. They were an uneasy bunch, trapped as they were, under water in the hands of the enemy. The general appearance of the Germans did not help matters. As Holbrook described them, they had "shaved their heads and allowed their beards to grow, so they looked like bearded sculpins or other strange creatures who would not only be ready to let blood, but willing to drink it, too." The U-boat commander Heinrich von Nostitz und Jänckendorff promised them they would be fairly treated and released when it was safe for the sub to do so.

Almost as soon as the two captive crews were taken aboard, U-151 was off again. The *Edna*, 325 tons, built in 1889 in Columbia Falls, Maine, and en route to Santiago from Philadelphia with a load of oil and gasoline, was attacked at about 4:00 p.m. In an account by Richard Hallet for the *Portland Sunday Telegram* in 1941, the *Edna*'s captain reacted similarly to Holbrook in that he also thought the sub's gunfire was from an American navy ship on maneuvers. He was soon advised differently by the U-boat captain who said, "Just get into your ship's boat and row over to the submarine…You'll find some of your friends over there." Then the *Edna* met the same fate as the other two ships, but the attempt to scuttle it failed. It was towed to shore some days later, as was the *Hauppage*, bottom side up. The *Dunn* took the first-place honors, as it was actually sunk.

When the *Edna*'s crew was brought aboard, something really bizarre took place. The *Edna*'s captain was Charles A. Gilmore of Tenants Harbor. Holbrook and Gilmore were childhood friends. They greeted each other enthusiastically, as they had not seen each other in thirty years; their lives at sea and times ashore at home had never coincided in all that time. Now, here they were both captured on the same day and imprisoned under water off New Jersey! Gilmore really did find a friend on board.

True to his promise, von Nostitz und Jänckendorff took care of his prisoners. They were bunked with the crew and officers and fed the same rations; they were even allowed on deck to stretch their legs. Again according to Hallet, "The politeness of the Germans soon got on everyone's nerves. Captain von Nostitz und Jänckendorff wanted everything done correct right down to the scratch of a pen…When he climbed over the *Edna*'s rail, he shook hands with the captain in the best German naval manner." It's a little galling to shake hands with your enemy like you were just bested in a sporting event. Even more galling, each American captain was given a written receipt for his ship.

## "BLACK SUNDAY"

Conditions were very crowded on the sub with twenty-three American prisoners, but it continued to go about its business. At one point, the sub lay on the seafloor near Chincoteague doing repairs. As Packard recounts, Holbrook said, "Ships propellers could be heard overhead, ships no doubt scouting for that very sub. It was pleasant to know that friends were only a couple of hundred feet away, but not so pleasant to think what might happen if discovered and a depth bomb dropped on it." One night, they surfaced and saw the lights of New York, reminding Holbrook that he had seen tickets to a Broadway show on the sub dated for the day before the *Hattie Dunn* was sunk. There really were no steps in place to prevent the U-boat crew from going on liberty in New York, no harbor protection or much in the line of patrols. U-151 did pretty much as it pleased. Along the way, the Germans cut underwater telegraph cables to Nova Scotia and laid mines only four miles from Cape Henlopen, Delaware, and two and a half miles southeast of the Overfalls Lightship. The sub was particularly equipped to lay mines and cut cables as part of its mission to disrupt trade and communications. For the time being, it sank no more ships.

Then, on June 2, 1918, nine days after sinking the *Hattie Dunn*, U-151 outdid itself by sinking six vessels in a single day: three sailing ships and three steamers off the Delaware and New Jersey coasts. Two others were damaged. This day quickly became known in the press as "Black Sunday." The following table shows the time and order of attacks. It is interesting to note that all the schooners and one of the steamers had connections to Maine. The table does not show that the third officer of the *Winneconne* was M.B. Brewer from Boothbay Harbor, who had formerly served as mate on the *Wiley*'s maiden voyage. The *New York Times* reported Brewer as saying, "When she sank, it seemed like killing an old friend."

## TABLE OF SHIPS SUNK BY U-151 ON BLACK SUNDAY, JUNE 2, 1918*

| Time/ Disposition | Ship Name | Type/ Tonnage | Date/Builder/Owner | Route | Cargo | Casualties |
|---|---|---|---|---|---|---|
| 7:50 a.m. Scuttled with bombs | *Isabel B. Wiley* | wooden schooner, 776 tons | 1906/New England SB Bath, ME/operated by Atlas Shipping, Philadelphia | Perth Amboy to Norfolk | Unknown | 0 |
| 9:12 a.m. Scuttled with bombs | *Winneconne* | steam freighter, 1,869 tons | 1907/Osbourne, Graham, Sunderland/Foreign Transport & Mercantile, NY | Boston to unknown | Unknown | 0 |
| 12:00 noon Shelled and scuttled with bombs | *Jacob M. Haskell* | wood-and-steel schooner, 1,798 tons | 1901/Cobb, Butler Co., Rockland, ME/Crowell and Thurber, Boston | Norfolk to Portland | Coal | 0 |
| 4:00 p.m. Scuttled with bombs | *Edward H. Cole* | wood-and-steel schooner, 1,791 tons | 1904/Cobb, Butler Co., Rockland, ME/Crowell and Thurber, Boston | Newport News to Portland | Coal | 0 |
| 5:20 p.m. Stopped by shelling, scuttled with bombs | *Texel* | steamer, 3,210 tons | 1913/in Rotteram/U.S. Shipping Board (the U.S. emergency agency that regulated the Shipping Act) | Puerto Rico to New York | Sugar | 0 |
| 7:20 p.m. Sunk by gunfire | *Carolina* | passenger steamer, 5,093 tons | 1896/in Newport News, VA/ New York and Porto Rico AA Co., Bath, ME | San Juan to New York | Passengers (218 men, women and children), Sugar | 13 (lifeboat overturned) |

*Sources: uboat.net and wrecksite.eu

All six boats were quickly run down, captured and sunk. No more prisoners could be taken on by the sub, so the crews of the newly captured ships were allowed to take to their lifeboats and make their own ways to safety. This also provided a way for the previously captured crews to be released. The *Winneconne* and *Wiley* lifeboats were told to pull up to the submarine, but instead of unloading, they took on the three prisoner crews. New York was a good sixty-five miles away; the crews rowed through the night and a thunderstorm until they were picked up and taken to New York. The next day, U-151 had another success; the *Herbert L. Pratt*, a 7,145-ton tanker loaded with oil, was damaged by the mines laid on May 27 near Cape Henlopen.

U-151 returned to Germany on July 20, 1918, without incident. Its voyage was a great (but not quite total) success in that it accomplished all of its missions. First, it helped prove the effectiveness of submarines that could readily travel to and from our Atlantic Coast and carry out war activities without the need to resupply while here. Next, it was able to disrupt coastal shipping and cause fear in Americans. It set mines and cut as many as three different telegraph cables. The actions of U-151 caused a blitz of news and complaints to the War Department but did not force the return of U.S. warships from Europe to defend the home coast, as Germany had hoped.

In the meantime, the navy questioned Holbrook and the other captains closely about their time on the sub, and the press had a field day with the stories as well. Americans obviously found the navy terribly remiss in not protecting American shores and merchantmen. The navy felt its first responsibility was to protect troop and supply ships crossing the Atlantic; this would be the surest way to win the war. However, this was the first attack on the American coast by another nation in one hundred years. The navy began to quickly implement long-planned measures for protecting the coast that had been neglected because the U-boat action was so totally (and implausibly) unexpected. Planes and dirigibles were put into use as sub spotters, and a more organized method of communicating ship movements was implemented. Convoying of ships was no longer recommended only to Europe but also along the coast. A new class of fast, small, wooden ships called sub chasers, first called for by assistant secretary of the navy Franklin D. Roosevelt in 1916, was put into more practical use along the East Coast to intercept U-boats.

## AFTERMATH

As soon as America entered the war, the *Prinz Eitel* was seized by the U.S. Navy. It was rechristened as the USS *DeKalb* and used as a troop ship. After the war, it was again repurposed, this time as the commercial liner SS *Mount Clay*. It was scrapped in 1935.

The news of the *Hattie Dunn*'s demise hit Dunn & Elliot hard. They were not only the ship's builders but also the managing owners. In addition, there were many local shareholders in Thomaston. After the war, they were able to recover about $60,000 for the loss of the vessel.

The U-151, built in Hamburg, Germany, in 1917, completed four patrols during the war, sunk thirty-four ships and damaged seven others. That's a total of 103,097 tons according to Uboat.net. It was surrendered at Cherbourg, France, at the close of the war and was used as a target ship there until it was sunk in 1921. Interestingly enough, Nazi Germany created a submarine namesake for U-151 in 1941 during World War II. The new U-151 made no patrols and damaged or sunk not a single ship. Instead, it was used as a training boat and was scuttled in May 1945 at Wilhelmshaven and eventually broken up.

There was another *William P. Frye* as well during World War II. The Liberty Class 441-foot-long *William Pierce Frye*, hull number 212, was built in the West Yard of the New England Shipbuilding Company in South Portland and launched in just three months on February 11, 1943. On its maiden voyage to Europe, it carried military stores, 750 tons of explosives and, like its namesake, wheat. A little over a month after its launch, it was separated from its convoy by a hurricane and by engine problems, and before it could catch up, the *Frye* was torpedoed by U-610. It went down fast. Only seven crewmen survived the attack, and then their real ordeal began. But that's another story.

# Bibliography

## Chapter 1

Baker, William Avery. *The Maritime History of Bath.* Bath, ME: Marine Research Society of Bath, 1973.

Banyard, Joseph, Richard Law Hinsdale and Alonzo Hartwell. *Plymouth and the Pilgrims; or, Incidents of Adventure in the History of the First Settlers.* Boston: Gould and Lincoln, 1851.

Baxter, James Phinney, and Ferdinando Gorges. *Sir Ferdinando Gorges and His Province of Maine. Including the Brief Relation, the Brief Narration, His Defense, the Charter Granted to Him, His Will, and His Letters.* Boston: Prince Society, 1967.

Bradford, William. 1901. Bradford's history "of Plimoth plantation." Boston: Wright & Potter Printing Co., n.d.

Burrage, Henry S. "The Plymouth Colonists in Maine." *Collections of the Maine Historical Society.* 3rd Series. Vol. 1. Portland: Maine Historical Society, 1904.

Chandler, E.J. *Ancient Sagadahoc.* 2nd Printing. N.p.: privately printed, 1997.

Cranmer, Leon. *Cushnoc: The History and Archaeology of Plymouth Colony Traders on the Kennebec.* Occasional publications of *Maine Archaeology*, no. 7. Augusta: Maine Historic Preservation, 1990.

Goodwin, John Abbot. *The Pilgrim Republic; an Historical Review of the Colony of New Plymouth.* Boston: Ticknor and Company, 1888.

Hatch, Louis. *Maine: A History.* Somersworth: New Hampshire Publishing Co., 1974.

McIntyre, Ruth A. *Debts Hopeful and Desperate: Financing the Plymouth Colony.* Plymouth, MA: Plimoth Plantation, 1963.

Nash, Charles Elventon. *The History of Augusta: First Settlements and Early Days as a Town.* Augusta, ME: Charles E. Nash and Sons, 1904.

North, James W. *The History of Augusta, Maine.* Somersworth, NH: New England History Press, 1981.

## CHAPTER 2

Cayford, John E. "The Sullivan Brothers." *Maine's Hall of Fame*. Brewer, ME: Cay-Bel Pub. Co., 1987.

Eaton, Cyrus. *History of Thomaston, Rockland, and South Thomaston, Maine, from Their First Exploration, A.D. 1605; with Family Genealogies*. Hallowell, ME: Masters, Smith, 1865.

Leamon, James S. *Revolution Downeast*. Amherst: University of Massachusetts Press, 1993.

Maine Writers Research Club. *Historic Churches and Homes of Maine*. Portland, ME: Falmouth Book House, 1937.

Morse, F.L.S. *Thomaston Scrapbook*. 2 vols. Thomaston, ME: Thomaston Historical Society, 1977.

Packard, Aubigne Lermond. *A Town That Went to Sea*. Portland, ME: Falmouth Publishing House, 1950.

Wadsworth, Peleg. "Letter from General Peleg Wadsworth to William D. Williamson, January 1, 1828." Maine Historical Society Collections, series 2, vol. 2, 153–62.

Wheeler, George Augustus, and Louise Wheeler Bartlett. *History of Castine, Penobscot and Brooksville, Maine*. Cornwall, NY: Cornwall Press, 1923.

Willis, William. *The History of Portland*. Somersworth: New Hampshire Publishing Co., 1972.

## CHAPTER 3

Cartland, John Henry. *Ten Years at Pemaquid; Sketches of Its History and Its Ruins*. N.p.: privately printed, 1899.

Chase, Fannie Scott. *Wiscasset in Pownalborough: A History of the Shire Town and the Salient Historical Features of the Territory between the Sheepscot and Kennebec Rivers*. Wiscasset, ME: Southworth-Anthoensen Press, 1941.

Crocker, Ken. Maine Maritime Museum. "Loose Cannon—or Don't Give Up the Provenence." *Rhumb Line* 69 (Summer 2012).

Department of the Navy. Naval History and Heritage Command. "Enterprise." *Dictionary of American Naval Fighting Ships*. http://www.history.navy.mil/danfs/e4/enterprise-iii.htm (accessed November 2013).

Goold, William. *Portland in the Past: With Historical Notes of Old Falmouth*. Bowie, MD: Heritage Books, 1997.

Picking, Sherwood. *Seafight Off Monhegan: The* Enterprise *and* Boxer. Portland, ME: Machigine Press, 1941.

Pratt, Fletcher. *Preble's Boys: Commodore Preble and the Birth of American Sea Power*. New York: Sloane, 1950.

Roberts, Kenneth. *Trending into Maine*. Boston: Little, Brown and Co, 1938.

Rumsey, Barbara. "Part III: The *Boxer* and the *Enterprise* Seafight in 1813." Wiscasset newspaper, November 16, 2012. http://www.wiscassetnewspaper.com/article/boxer-and-enterprise-sea-fight-1813-part-iii/5850 (accessed November 2013).

———. "Part II: The *Boxer* and the *Enterprise* Seafight in 1813." Wiscasset newspaper, October 30, 2012. http://www.wiscassetnewspaper.com/article/part-ii-boxer-and-enterprise-sea-fight-1813/5040 (accessed November 2013).
———. "What Remains of the *Boxer* and the *Enterprise* Seafight, Part 1." *Boothbay Register*, October 13, 2013. http://www.boothbayregister.com/article/what-remains-1813-boxer-and-enterprise-sea-fight/20640 (accessed November 2013).

## CHAPTER 4

Burrage, Henry S., Kenneth C.M. Sills and Augustus Freedom Moulton. *Maine Historical Memorials*. Augusta, ME: printed for the state, 1922.
Hatch, Louis Clinton. *Maine: A History*. New York: American Historical Society, 1919.
Humiston, Fred S. *Blue Water Men and Women*. Portland, ME: G. Gannett Pub. Co., 1965.
Packard, Aubigne Lermond. *A Town That Went to Sea*. Portland, ME: Falmouth Pub. House, 1950.
Schriver, Edward O. *Go Free: The Antislavery Impulse in Maine, 1833–1855*. Orono: University of Maine Press, 1970.
Thomas, Miriam Stover, Steven J. Bentley and Thomas Shaw Henley. *Flotsam and Jetsam*. Maine: S.J. Bentley and T.S. Henley, 1998.

## CHAPTER 5

Anderson, Eve, Jonathan Cilley and Deborah Prince Cilley. A Breach of Privilege: Cilley Family Letters, 1820–1867. Spruce Head, ME: Seven Coin Press, 2002.
CLERKWEB. *Biographical Directory of the United States Congress 1774–Present*. http://bioguide.congress.gov (accessed November 2013).
Cochran, Hamilton. *Noted American Duels and Hostile Encounters*. New York: Chilton Books, 1963.
Eaton, Cyrus. *History of Thomaston, Rockland, and South Thomaston, Maine, from Their First Exploration, A.D. 1605; with Family Genealogies*. Hallowell, ME: Masters, Smith, 1865.
Hatch, Louis. *Maine: A History*. Somersworth: New Hampshire Publishing Co., 1973.
Hawthorne, Nathaniel. "Jonathan Cilley." 1838. http://www.eldritchpress.org/nh/cily.html (accessed November 2013).
King, Horatio. "History of the Duel between Jonathan Cilley and William J. Graves." Maine Historical Society Collections, series 2, vol. 3 (1892): 127–48.
Seitz, Don C. *Famous American Duels*. Freeport, NY: Books for Libraries Press, 1966.
Stall, Buddy. "A Dueling Loophole: Harpoons at 20 Paces." *Clarion Herald*, September 16, 1999.
Taylor, Troy. "Haunted Maryland: The Bladensburg Dueling Grounds." Bladensburg, MD. 1998. http://www.prairieghosts.com/bladensburg.html (accessed November 2013).
Watson, S.M. "Jonathan Cilley of Maine and William J. Graves of Kentucky, Representatives in Congress, an Historical Duel, 1838, as Narrated by Gen.

George R. Jones, Cilley's Second to E.M. Boyle, in Philadelphia Press." *Maine Historical and Genealogical Recorder* 6, no. 3 (1884).

## CHAPTER 6

Davis, Jefferson. *The Project Gutenberg EBook of Speeches of the Honorable Jefferson Davis*. 1858. Last modified May 18, 2003, http:www2.cddc.vt.edu/gutenberg/etext04/sphjd10h.htm.

Davis, Varina H. *Jefferson Davis: A Memoir by His Wife*. New York: Belford Co. Publishers, 1890.

Hussey, Terry. The Base Line Across the Blueberry Barrens and Its Most Important Visitor. Milbridge Historical Society. http://www.milbridgehistoricalsociety.org (accessed November 2013).

Rowland, Eron. *Varina Howell, Wife of Jefferson Davis*. New York: Macmillan Co., 1927.

Stahl, Jasper Jacob. *The Nineteenth and Twentieth Centuries.* Volume 2 in *The History of Old Broad Bay and Waldoboro.* Portland, ME: Bond Wheelwight Company, 1956.

Strode, Hudson. *Jefferson Davis: American Patriot 1808–1861*. New York: Harcourt, Brace and Company, 1955.

Theberge, Albert E. The Coast Survey, 1806–1867. NOAA. Last modified November 30, 2007. http://www.lib.noaa.gov/noaainfo/heritage/coastsurveyvol1/TITLE.html.

Vose, Caroline E. "When Bowdoin College Conferred the LL.D Degree on Jeferson Davis." In *A Distant War Comes Home: Maine in the Civil War Era*. Camden, ME: Down East Books, 1996.

## CHAPTER 7

Catton, Bruce. *Grant Takes Command*. Boston: Little, Brown, 1968.

Civil War Society. "Civil War Medicine: Medical Care, Battle Wounds, and Disease." *Encyclopedia of the Civil War*. Last updated February 10, 2002. http://www.civilwarhome.com/civilwarmedicine.htm.

Damariscotta Historical Society. "Two Right Arms." *Lincoln County Weekly*, April 18, 2004.

Desjardin, Thomas A. *Stand Firm Ye Boys from Maine: The 20th Maine and the Gettysburg Campaign*. Gettysburg, PA: Thomas Publications, 1995.

Goellnitz, Jenny. eHistory. Civil War Battlefield Medicine. http://www.civilwarmedicine.aphillcsa.com (accessed November 2013).

Houston, Henry Clarence. *The Thirty-second Maine Regiment of Infantry Volunteers: An Historical Sketch*. Portland, ME: Press of Southworth Bros, 1903.

National Park Service. "The Crater—Petersburg National Battlefield." Last modified October 31, 2013. http://www.nps.gov/pete/historyculture/the-crater.htm.

Pullen, John J. *A Shower of Stars: The Medal of Honor and the 27th Maine*. Philadelphia: Lippincott, 1966.

———. *The Twentieth Maine: A Volunteer Regiment in the Civil War*. Dayton, OH: Morningside House, 1957.

Whitman, William E.S., and Charles Henry True. *Maine in the War for the Union: A History of the Part Borne by Maine Troops in the Suppression of the American Rebellion*. Lewiston, ME: N. Dingley Jr. & Co., 1865.

Woodward, Joseph T. *Historic Record and Complete Biographic Roster, 21st Me. Vols. with Reunion Records of the 21st Maine Regimental Association*. Augusta, ME: Press of C.E. Nash and Son, 1907.

## CHAPTER 8

Baker, William Avery. *The Maritime History of Bath*. Bath, ME: Marine Research Society of Bath, 1973.

*Bangor Semi-weekly News*. "The *Eitel* to Stay Until War Is Over." March 16, 1915, 6, col. 6.

Cruikshank, Jeffery L., and Chloe G. Kline. *In Peace and War: A History of the U.S. Merchant Marine Academy at Kings Point.*. Hoboken, NJ: John Wiley & Sons, 2008.

"Destruction of American Merchantman *William P. Frye* by the German Ship *Prinz Eitel Friedrich*." *American Journal of International Law*, no. 4 (1916): 345–353. http://www.jstor.org/stable/2212614 (accessed November 2013).

Fairburn, William. *Merchant Sail*. Vol. 3. Center Lovell, ME: Fairburn Marine Educational Foundation, 1945.

Galiano, Rich. "'Black Sunday'—Victims of U-151." Last modified April 28, 2009. http://njscuba.net/sites/site_black_sunday.html.

Hallet, Richard Matthews. Submarines of World War I Off the Maine Coast. 1941.

Kurd, Archibald. *The Merchant Navy*. London: John Murray, 1921.

Lubbock, Basil. *The Down Easters: American Deep-Water Sailing Ships 1869–1929*. Glasgow: Brown, Son & Ferguson, 1929.

*New York Times*. "Germany Agrees to Pay for Frye." April 9, 1915. http://query.nytimes.com/mem/archive-free/pdf?res=FA0D17F83F5C15738DDDA00894DC405B858DF1D3 (accessed November 2013).

———. "U-boat Prisoners Arrive." June 4, 1918. http://query.nytimes.com/mem/archive-free/pdf?res=F70C17F83D5A11738DDDAD0894DE405B888DF1D3 (accessed November 2013).

Packard, Aubigne Lermond. *A Town That Went to Sea*. Portland, ME: Falmouth Publishing House, 1950.

U-boat.net. "The U-boat in World War I." http://uboat.net/wwi (accessed November 2013).

The Wreck Site. "*Hattie Dunn* (1918)." Last modified October 22, 2009. http://www.wrecksite.eu/wreck.aspx?150783.

———. "*William P. Frye* ( 1915)." Last modified August 29, 2011. http://www.wrecksite.eu/wreck.aspx?163169.

# About the Author

Pat Higgins was born in Maine and has lived here all her life except for a few years spent elsewhere by accident. She is a graduate of the University of Southern Maine with a BA in history and of the University of Rhode Island with a master's in library and information science. She worked as a school librarian for more than thirty years, serving grades from kindergarten through college. Now retired, Pat likes to garden, knit, paint and read. Occasionally, when an interesting little story comes up, she likes to investigate and write it up. She and her husband, Dave, live on the Midcoast and love every minute of it.

www.ingramcontent.com/pod-product-compliance
Lightning Source LLC
LaVergne TN
LVHW010937100826
845153LV00001B/75

* 9 7 8 1 5 4 0 2 2 3 0 4 3 *